State v. Sanchez

Case File

Trial Materials

Third Edition

STATE V. SANCHEZ

Case File

Trial Materials

Third Edition

Elizabeth I. Boals
Associate Professor of Law
Director, Center for Excellence in Advocacy
Stetson University College of Law

NITA®
NATIONAL INSTITUTE FOR TRIAL ADVOCACY

Address inquiries to:
Reprint Permission
National Institute for Trial Advocacy
325 W. South Boulder Rd., Ste. 1
Louisville, CO 80027-1130
Phone: (800) 225-6482
Email: publications@nita.org

ISBN 979-8-886-69061-3
FBA 2061
eISBN 979-8-886-69062-0
eFBA 2062

Printed in the United States of America

ASPEN PUBLISHING

Official co-publisher of NITA.
aspenpublishing.com/NITA

Contents

Electronic, color versions of exhibits can be found at the following website:

http://bit.ly/1P20Jea
Password: Sanchez3

ACKNOWLEDGMENTS

The author would like to acknowledge the special contributions made by Cameron Sargent and Rylie Pennell, Stetson University College of Law students, who assisted with editing this case file.

Also, thanks to my husband, Tim Boals, for his constant encouragement and willingness to pose as the deceased for the photographs used in this case file.

Introduction

This case file contains materials for the trial of a defendant charged with murder and participation in a criminal street gang. These materials provide users with opportunities to consider criminal trial issues, including the defense of self-defense, lesser included offenses, testimony of non-traditional experts (in the area of gangs), evidence in the form of digital recordings and "Flashgram" messages, and impeachment by inconsistent statement in a witness-sponsored website.

This case file also addresses the potential impact of racial bias during a criminal trial. Though these topics can be politically and emotionally charged, the issue of race plays prominently in most gang-related prosecutions. Racial bias, however, is often also present in non-gang-related prosecutions. This case file allows users to deal, in a safe environment, with the potential racial bias of witnesses and jurors in their strategic case planning, examination of witnesses, opening statements, and closing arguments.

The author hopes that this case file will familiarize attorneys with the many challenges that are an integral part of the preparation and presentation of criminal cases in modern courts of law.

Case Summary

A grand jury charged Ernesto Sanchez under the Nita Criminal Code with first-degree murder and participation in a criminal street gang in the stabbing death of Patrick Connor on March 10, YR-1. The stabbing took place in the parking lot in front of Fisher's Convenience Store and Restaurant near the intersection of Old State Pike and Norton Road in Nita City. Victor Buentello has been granted immunity from prosecution on these same charges in exchange for his cooperation in a federal prosecution of an unrelated matter.

Mr. Sanchez and Mr. Buentello have known each other since childhood but are not close friends. They grew up in the same neighborhood and have friends in common. On the morning of March 10, YR-1, Mr. Sanchez and Mr. Buentello walked together to Putnam Park to play basketball. They arrived at the park around noon; pickup basketball games were already in progress. After playing basketball for approximately three hours with several other men, Mr. Sanchez left. He walked north on Norton Road toward Fisher's Convenience Store and Restaurant, which is located at the intersection of Norton Road and Old State Pike. Mr. Buentello left shortly after with another man who had also participated in the basketball games. Mr. Buentello and his companion were walking in the same direction approximately thirty yards behind Mr. Sanchez.

A group of people were gathered in front of Fisher's Convenience Store, which is located next to Fisher's Restaurant. Many of the people in this group were wearing red and white clothing. Red and white are the colors of Las Calaveras, a local street gang. Many, if not all, of the people in this group were Las Calaveras gang members. A person in the group called Mr. Sanchez over to the group. As Mr. Sanchez entered the group, several vehicles pulled up, and several suspected members of the Stone Cross gang emerged. A fight broke out. During the fight, Mr. Sanchez stabbed Patrick Connor once in the chest. Mr. Connor was a suspected member of the Stone Cross gang. He was pronounced dead at the scene. Mr. Buentello was holding Mr. Connor at the time of the stabbing. Mr. Sanchez and Mr. Buentello fled the scene.

Mr. Sanchez and Mr. Buentello gave statements to the police. Mr. Sanchez claimed he was acting in self-defense when he stabbed Mr. Connor. Mr. Buentello claimed that he was acting in defense of Mr. Sanchez when he held Mr. Connor during the stabbing.

The applicable law is contained in the statutes and proposed jury instructions set forth at the end of this case file.

All years in these materials are stated in the following form:

YR-0 indicates the actual year in which the case is being tried (i.e., the present year); YR-1 indicates the next preceding year (please use the actual year); YR-2 indicates the second preceding year (please use the actual year), etc.

Electronic, color versions of exhibits can be found at the following website:

http://bit.ly/1P20Jea
Password: Sanchez3

Instructions

Unless otherwise instructed, a party need not call all the witnesses on their list. Except for Mr. Sanchez, who may be called only in his own defense, either party may call any or all of the witnesses.

State:	Detective Terry Hefler
	Dr. Lee Taylor
	Lieutenant Jamie Delgado
	Mary Kelly
	Martin Salas
Defense:	Ernesto Sanchez
	Victor Buentello
	Pat Donahue
	Chris Cavallo
	Luis Ambrose

REQUIRED STIPULATIONS

1) The butterfly knife found at the scene was fingerprinted by the Nita State Laboratory. Ernesto Sanchez's fingerprints were the only fingerprints found on the butterfly knife.

2) The blood samples from the butterfly knife, the ground under the knife, and the ground under the deceased's body were tested by the Nita State Laboratory. The blood found in these three locations was Patrick Connor's blood.

3) The FBI criminal records for Victor Buentello and Pat Donahue are accurate and authentic.

4) The certified criminal convictions of Victor Buentello are true and accurate copies of his conviction. They have been properly certified by the clerk's office for the District Court of Nita City. These certified copies, if relevant, are admissible without the testimony of the custodian of the records pursuant to Nita Criminal Code Section 1-10-101.

5) Las Calaveras is a criminal street gang as defined by Nita Criminal Code Section 2-18-101(a).

6) On March 10 at about 3:40 p.m., Ernesto Sanchez was interviewed by the local news station. Mr. Sanchez willingly agreed to speak about the fight on the condition that his face was not shown on camera. Exhibit 24 is the digital recording of this interview. Exhibit 24 is an accurate, authentic, and complete digital recording of the interview. (The digital recording is available at http://bit.ly/1P20Jea, Password: Sanchez3.)

7) Ernesto Sanchez has a Flash account under the handle "@putnamparkneto." On March 10, YR-1, at 3:41 and 3:42 p.m., Mr. Sanchez sent two separate Flashgram messages. Exhibits 25 and 26 are accurate, authentic, and complete copies of those Flashgram messages.

8) The Heart 24/7 app screenshots reflected in Exhibit 42 are true and accurate depictions of the trip files as they appear on Mr. Sanchez's phone. The Heart 24/7 app contained other trip records for February and March YR-1. The parties stipulate the other records are not relevant to this case.

NOTE: The defense made a motion to suppress the March 16, YR-1, photo spread identification of Ernesto Sanchez by Mary Kelly. The court denied the motion.

NITA STATUTES

Nita Criminal Code—Chapter 1

Section 1-10-101. Admissibility of Certified Court Records

The records of any judicial proceeding and any other official records of court, if otherwise admissible, shall be received into evidence without the testimony of the record's custodian, provided that such records are authenticated and certified by the clerk of the court having legal custody of the record.

Nita Criminal Code—Chapter 2

Section 2-2-101. Murder in the First Degree

A person who kills a human being in a premeditated, deliberate, and willful manner commits murder in the first degree.

Section 2-2-102. Murder in the Second Degree

a) A person who kills a human being with either the intent to kill or the intent to inflict such serious bodily harm that death would be the likely result commits murder in the second degree.

b) Second-degree murder does not require premeditation or deliberation.

Section 2-2-103. Manslaughter

A person who kills another human being without malice aforethought but either with intent to kill or with conscious disregard for human life is guilty of voluntary manslaughter. There is no malice aforethought if the killing occurred upon a sudden quarrel or heat of passion or in the actual but unreasonable belief in the necessity to defend oneself or another person against imminent peril to life or great bodily injury.

Section 2-18-101. Participation in a Criminal Street Gang

a) Definitions

"Criminal street gang," as it appears in § 2-18-101(b), means any organization of three or more persons with the following two characteristics:

1) having as one of its activities the commission of one or more of the following criminal acts:

   A) unlawful homicide or manslaughter;

   B) robbery;

   C) assault with a deadly weapon;

   D) rape;

   E) the sale or possession for sale of controlled substances; and

2) having a common name or common identifying sign or symbol.

"Pattern of criminal gang activity," as it appears in § 2-18-101(b), means the commission of or attempted commission of two or more of the following crimes:

1) unlawful homicide or manslaughter;

2) robbery;

3) assault with a deadly weapon;

4) rape;

5) the sale or possession for sale of controlled substances.

"Active participation," as it appears in § 2-18-101(b), means that the person must have a relationship with the criminal street gang that is more than passive or inactive.

b) Participation in a Criminal Street Gang

A person commits the crime of participation in a criminal street gang if they actively participate in a criminal street gang with knowledge that the members engaged in, or have engaged in, a pattern of criminal gang activity, and they willfully promote, further, or assist in any felonious criminal conduct by members of that gang.

Section 2-29-101. Exemption from Criminal Responsibility: Self-Defense and Defense of Others

a) A person is justified in using physical force upon another person in order to defend themself or a third person from what they reasonably believe to be the use or imminent use of unlawful physical force by that other person, and may use a degree of force that they reasonably believe to be necessary for that purpose.

b) Deadly physical force may be used only if a person reasonably believes a lesser degree of force is inadequate, and the actor has reasonable ground to believe, and does believe, that they or another person is in imminent danger of being killed or receiving great bodily harm.

c) Notwithstanding the provisions of subsection (a), a person is not justified in using physical force if:

   1) with intent to cause physical injury or death to another person, they provoke the use of unlawful physical force by that other person; or

   2) the person is the initial aggressor.

Section 2-22-101. Principal in the Second Degree: Aiding and Abetting

a) Definitions

For purposes of this section only, the term "principal" means an individual who has been charged with a crime.

b) Principal in the second degree

A person is a principal in the second degree if that person aids and abets a principal in the commission of a crime by:

1) knowingly associating in some way with the crime; and
2) intentionally participating in the crime by committing some act designed to help the crime succeed.

c) Punishment

A principal in the second degree, under this section, is guilty of the underlying offense committed by the principal.

Section 2-43-101. Unlawful Carrying of a Concealed Weapon

A person commits the offense of unlawful carrying of a concealed weapon when they knowingly carry about their person, unless in an open manner and fully exposed to view, any bludgeon, metal knuckles, firearm, knife with a blade longer than four inches, or any other dangerous or deadly weapon or instrument of like character outside of the person's home or place of business.

CASE MATERIALS AND EXHIBITS

Electronic, color versions of exhibits can be found at the following website:

http://bit.ly/1P20Jea
Password: Sanchez3

IN THE DISTRICT COURT
FOR THE CITY OF NITA

THE PEOPLE OF THE STATE OF NITA	)	
	)	
v.	)	Case No. CR 3711
	)	
ERNESTO P. SANCHEZ,	)	INDICTMENT
	)	
Defendant.	)	

The Grand Jury in and for the City of Nita, State of Nita, upon their oath and in the name and by the authority of the State of Nita, does hereby charge the following offenses under the criminal code of the State of Nita:

COUNT I

That on March 10, YR-1, at and within the City of Nita in the State of Nita, Ernesto P. Sanchez committed the crime of

MURDER IN THE FIRST DEGREE

in violation of Section 2-2-101 of the Nita Criminal Code of 1974, as amended, in that he killed another human being, namely Patrick J. Connor, in a premeditated, deliberate, and willful manner contrary to the form of the Statute and against the peace and dignity of the People of the State of Nita.

COUNT II

That on March 10, YR-1, at and within the City of Nita in the State of Nita, Ernesto P. Sanchez committed the crime of

PARTICIPATION IN A CRIMINAL STREET GANG

in violation of Section 2-18-101 of the Nita Criminal Code of 1974, as amended, in that he actively participated in a criminal street gang with knowledge that the members engaged in, or have engaged in, a pattern of criminal gang activity and willfully promoted, furthered, or assisted in felonious criminal conduct by members of that gang contrary to the form of the statute and against the peace and dignity of the People of the State of Nita.

Exhibit 1

Police Report, 3-10-YR-1, Initial Report

STATE OF NITA **NARRATIVE REPORT** NPR 5490 (Rev. 07-YR-10) OPI D87				Page 1 of 2
Date of Incident/Occurrence 03-10-YR-1	Time 3:00 PM	NCIC Number 68474	Officer I.D. Number 2653	Number 000YR-1-056
"X" One ☒ Narrative ☐ Supplemental	"X" One ☒ Criminal report ☐ Other	Type Supplemental ("X" Applicable) ☐ Collision Update ☐ Fatal ☐ Hit and Run Update ☐ Hazardous materials ☐ School bus☐ Other ______		
City/County/Judicial District Nita City/Darrow/First			Reporting District/Beat Putnam Park	Citation Number N/A
Location/Subject Fisher's Convenience Store, 679 Old State Pike			State Highway Related ☐ Yes ☒ No	

NARRATIVE:

Officer Background: I earned an associate degree in criminal justice from Nita University in YR-11 and graduated from the Nita Police Academy (six-month program) in YR-10. For the past ten years, I have been assigned to patrol the Putnam Park area. I have attended the standard courses on crime scene preservation and evidence collection and maintenance that the Nita City Police Department offers. These courses consisted of approximately sixteen hours per year of classroom lecture and sixteen hours per year of supervised field work.

On March 10, YR-1, at approximately 3:00 p.m., I was in my vehicle on routine patrol around the Putnam Park area. Putnam Park is part of my regular patrol because of the high level of gang activity. I was at the southwest corner of the park by the basketball courts when I received a call from the dispatcher that there was a gang fight at Fisher's Convenience Store. I activated my lights and siren and headed to the intersection of Norton Road and Old State Pike. It took me approximately three minutes to arrive at the scene. I arrived at the scene at the same time as two other police vehicles.

There was a crowd of people in the area. They were gathered in the parking lot in front of Fisher's Convenience Store and across Old State Pike in the front yard of the residence at 680 Old State Pike. By the time I arrived, the fight had dissipated. I could see a white male lying on the pavement in front of Fisher's Convenience Store. He was not moving. He was lying on his side with his back toward me. I could not see his hands. I approached with caution and shouted for him to show his hands. He didn't respond. I put my hand on him, and he didn't respond. I rolled him on his back. His right hand was pressed to his chest. I could see he was bleeding from the chest. He was not breathing and had no pulse. I did not perform CPR because of his chest wound. Emergency personnel arrived a minute later. They pronounced him dead at the scene. A representative from the coroner's office claimed the body.

I secured the area and searched for weapons. The only weapon found was a butterfly knife. The knife was located about a foot from the victim's right foot. It had what appeared to be blood on the blade. I secured it in an evidence bag with my initials on the label and locked it in the evidence locker in the trunk of my vehicle. I searched the area for blood evidence, but the composition of the parking lot (poorly maintained asphalt and gravel) made it difficult to locate blood evidence. I was only able to locate two drops of blood directly under the knife and a small pool of blood under the victim's body. I took samples of the two blood drops and the pool of blood with the police department issued blood collection kit. I secured the samples in an evidence bag with my initials on the label and locked it in the evidence locker in the trunk of my vehicle. After leaving the scene, I transported the evidence bags to the evidence room at the police station where they were logged in and secured. There was no blood spatter evidence.

I photographed the body as it appeared when I rolled it over and generated a diagram of the neighborhood. The diagram is to scale except that Putnam Park Elementary is larger than it appears in the diagram. Both are attached.

Preparer's Name, Rank, Division, and I.D. Number	Date
Hefler, Terry, Detective, Street Enforcement Unit, 2653	***03-10-YR-1***

YR-10 654613

Exhibit 1 (cont.)

Police Report, 3-10-YR-1, Initial Report

State of Nita
Narrative Report
NPR 5490 (Rev. 07-YR-10) OPI D87

Page 2 of 2

Date of Incident/Occurrence	Time	NCIC Number	Officer I.D. Number	Number
03-10-YR-1	3:00 PM	68474	2653	000YR-1-056
"X" One ☒ Narrative ☐ Supplemental	"X" One ☒ Criminal report ☐ Other ______	Type Supplemental ("X" Applicable) ☐ Collision Update ☐ Fatal ☐ Hit and Run Update ☐ Hazardous materials ☐ School bus☐ Other ______		
City/County/Judicial District Nita City/Darrow/First			Reporting District/Beat Putnam Park	Citation Number N/A
Location/Subject Fisher's Convenience Store, 679 Old State Pike			State Highway Related ☐ Yes ☒ No	

After securing the area, I questioned approximately ten people around the scene. Three individuals claimed they witnessed the fight: Mary Kelly, Martin Salas, and Chris Cavallo. Their statements are attached. I spoke with Luis Ambrose, owner of Fisher's Restaurant. He said that he wanted to talk to me about the incident but that it would have to be tomorrow because the restaurant was too busy for him to talk that evening.

Preparer's Name, Rank, Division, and I.D. Number	Date
Hefler, Terry, Detective, Street Enforcement Unit, 2653	***03-10-YR-1***

YR-10 654613

Exhibit 2

Diagram of Scene

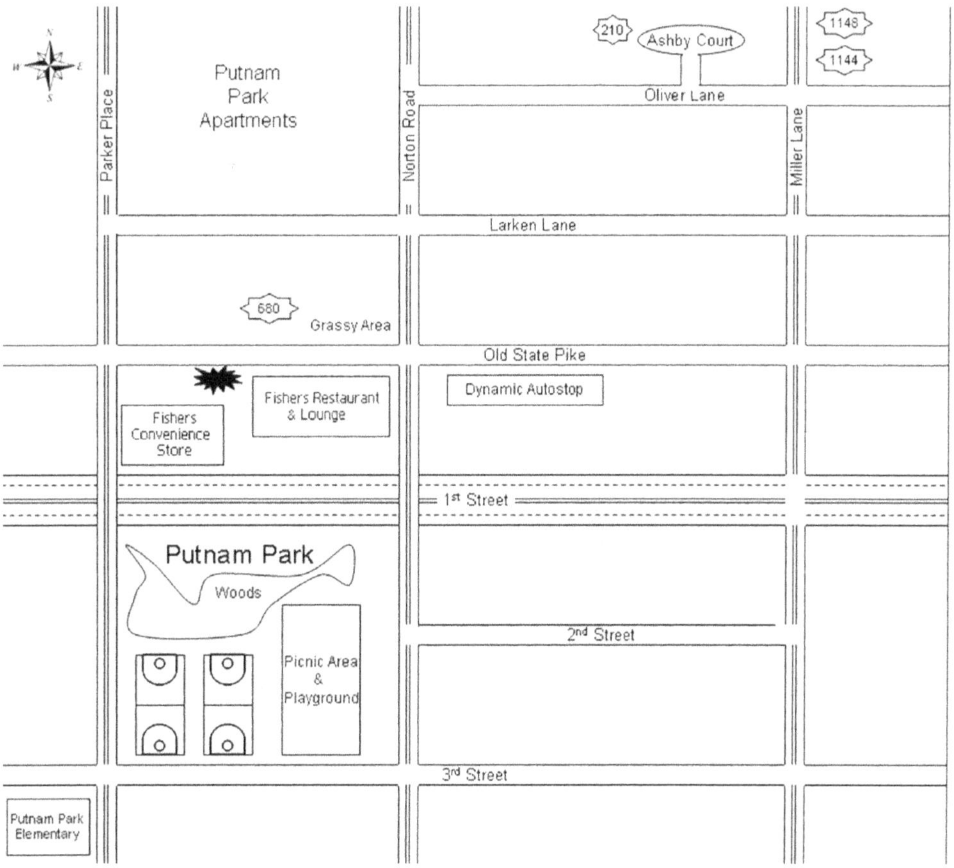

03-10-YR-1 Report Supplement, Detective Terry Hefler

Exhibit 3

PHOTO OF BODY (1)

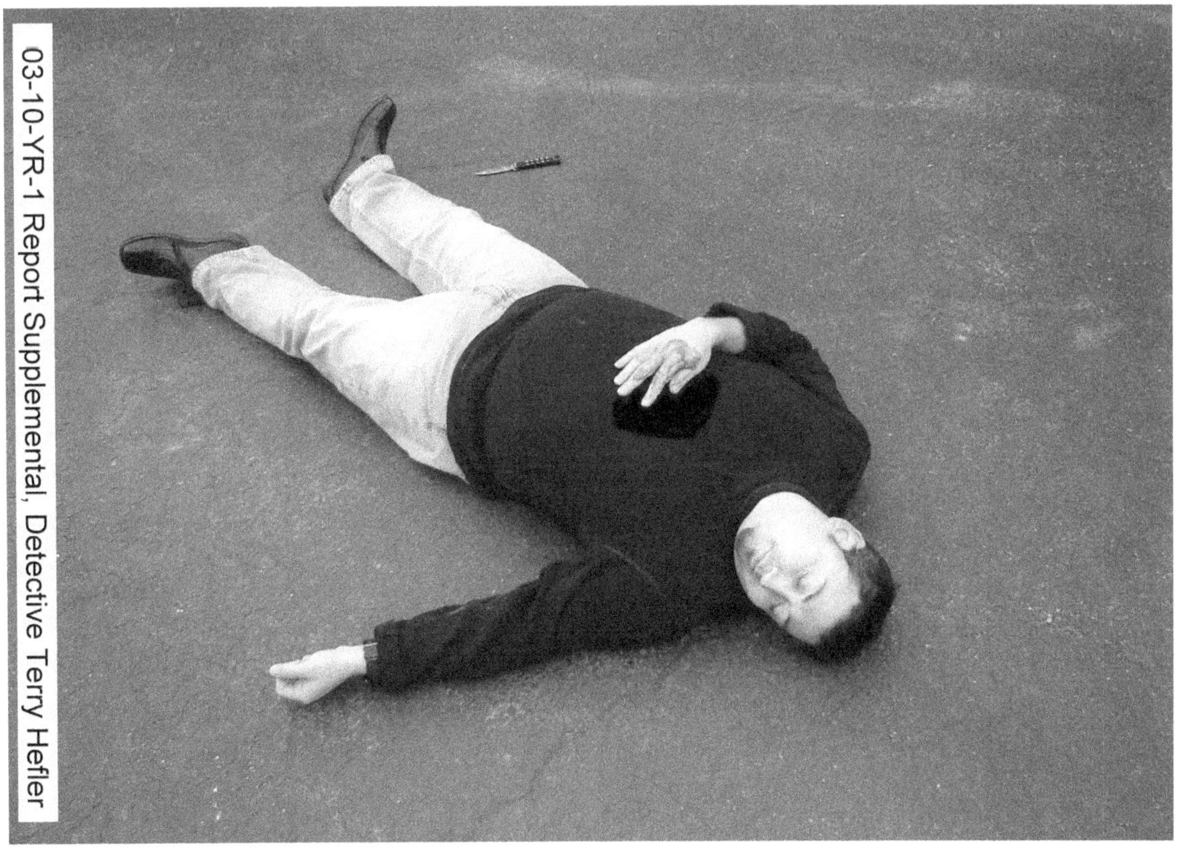

Exhibit 4

Photo of Body (2)

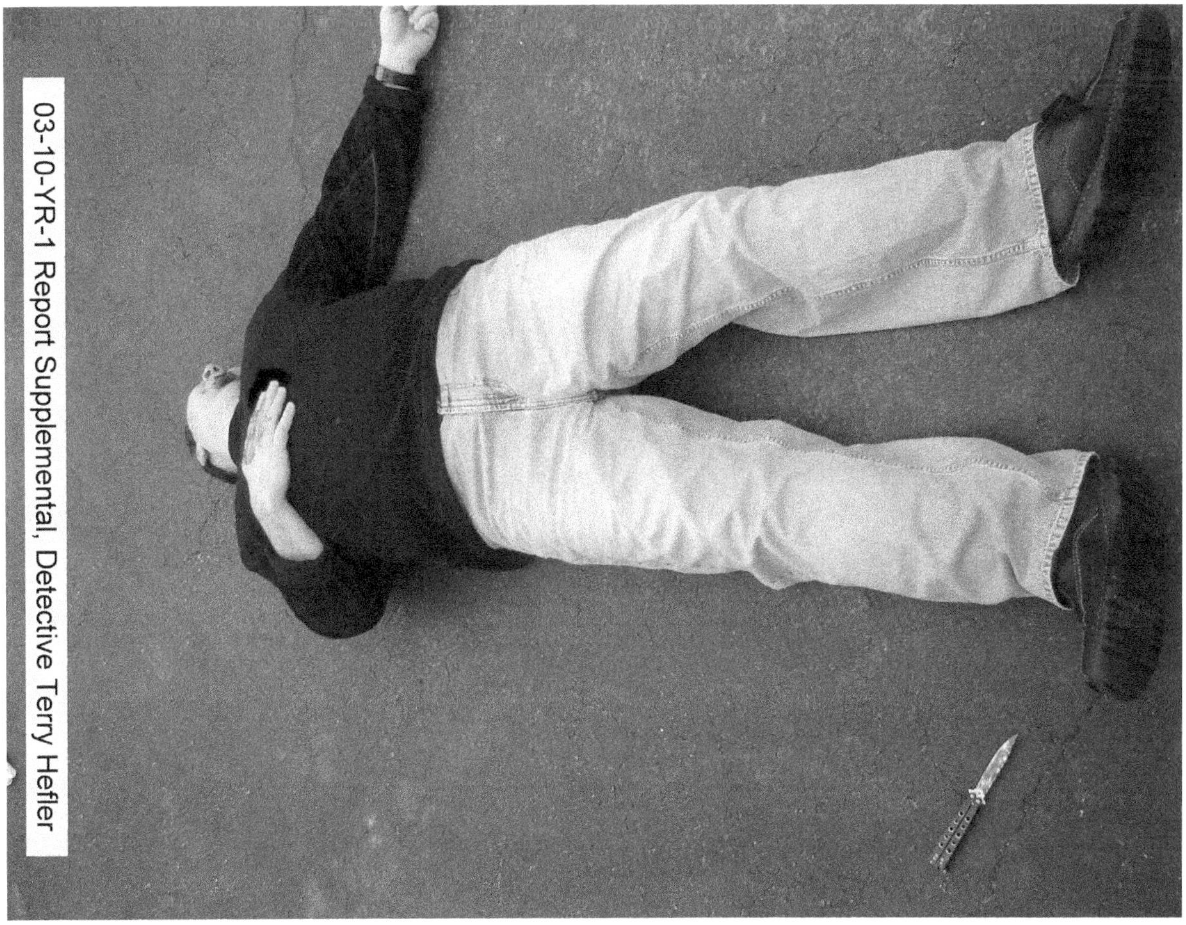

Exhibit 5

Photo of Knife (1)

Exhibit 6

PHOTO OF KNIFE (2)

Statement of Mary Kelly

Detective Hefler asked me to come to the Nita City Police Department and write a statement about what I saw in the Fisher's Convenience Store parking lot on March 10, YR-1. This is my statement.

My name is Mary A. Kelly. I was born on November 11, YR-30. I live at 680 Old State Pike. I live with my coworker, Sarah Collins. I don't have any children. I have lived with Sarah in this rental house for seven years. We work at Putnam Park Elementary, which is located about four blocks from the house on the other side of the park. I teach third grade.

My neighborhood was a quiet suburb on the fringe of the Nita City limits until approximately five years ago, when there was an increase in minorities moving into the neighborhood. I have nothing against Latinos or any other ethnic group, but with these groups came the gangs. We did not have a gang problem until the Latinos arrived.

Now there are lots of fights in my neighborhood, so it didn't surprise me when I heard people shouting outside Fisher's Convenience Store on March 10, YR-1. I was in my living room in the front of my house when I first heard loud voices. I couldn't make out what they were saying. My roommate had walked over to the convenience store a few minutes earlier. When I heard the loud voices, I was concerned something would happen to her, so I walked out the front door and across my front yard to see what the commotion was about. I was about halfway across my front yard when I stopped to watch the fight across the street in the parking lot of the convenience store. There were about thirty people involved. I scanned the fight for Sarah. I spotted her standing in the front door of the convenience store with some other bystanders. She seemed all right.

Las Calaveras is the Latino gang that runs my neighborhood. They are a rough, crude bunch. I try to keep my distance from them. Sometimes they harass Sarah and me when we walk through the park on our way home from work. They also cut through our yard to get to Fisher's Convenience Store. They have no respect for anyone. Any Latino in our neighborhood who is wearing red and white is bad news. The March 10 fight involved Las Calaveras. I don't know any of them personally, but I could tell from all the red and white that they were Las Calaveras. There were approximately twenty of them involved in the fight.

While I was scanning the crowd for Sarah, I witnessed the murder. I saw a big guy in a black shirt with something in his hand, maybe a baseball bat or stick, raising his arms up over his head and walking toward this Las Calaveras guy who was on his knees. The guy on his knees was wearing a red and white shirt. There were a bunch of people around the guy on his knees, but I didn't see how the guy ended up on his knees. This was happening about fifty yards from where I was standing. There was nothing in between me and these guys except maybe a few cars that drove by on Old State Pike. When the big guy with the bat or stick was about three feet from the Las Calaveras guy who was on his knees, a second Las Calaveras guy grabbed him from behind. He grabbed the big guy's arms and pulled them back over the guy's head. They struggled for a second or two. I think the big guy dropped the bat or whatever he was holding. The first Las Calaveras guy who was on his knees got up from the ground. I thought he was going to punch the guy or something like that, but instead he lunged at the restrained guy and drove a small knife into his chest. He was holding the knife underhand and just sort of stuck it in straight. I think the knife was in his left hand, but I am not sure. It wasn't a big knife. The big guy crumbled to the ground. I had a clear view of the stabber's face, but I did not get a good look at the guy that held the victim because his back was to me. The two Las Calaveras guys ran after the victim hit the ground. Right then this small Las Calaveras guy yelled, "Las Calaveras rules." It was a horrific thing to watch. About a minute later I heard sirens, and everyone ran.

I recognized the guy with the knife from the neighborhood. He is in his early twenties, medium complexion, dark hair and eyes. I doubt that my description will help you much. I know I could pick him out of a lineup because I recognize him from the neighborhood. He's one of those thugs who cuts through my yard, and I've also seen him hanging around with that Las Calaveras bunch. I think I also saw him in the Fisher's Convenience Store parking lot a few weeks ago. I think he was casing cars to steal them. He was just standing against the building looking at the cars in the parking lot. He was standing there for at least fifteen minutes (as long as it took me to do some shopping in the convenience store). I am sure he was up to something illegal.

After the fight, I waited until the police came to tell them what I saw. Sarah says that I am stupid for getting involved, but I feel it is my civic duty. I also just got a new job at a private school in Washington, DC. I am moving to DC in a month. Las Calaveras is a local gang, so I'm not really worried about retribution.

I will come back to testify if someone pays for my airfare and lodging.

I have read this statement, and it is a true and accurate account of what I witnessed in the Fisher's Convenience Store parking lot on March 10, YR-1.

This statement was written and signed by the witness in the presence of Detective Terry Hefler.

Mary A. Kelly

Mary A. Kelly

March 10, YR-1

Date

Statement of Chris Cavallo

Detective Hefler interviewed me at the incident scene and, with my mother's permission, transported me to the Nita City Police Department to write and sign this statement about what I saw in the Fisher's Convenience Store parking lot on March 10, YR-1.

My name is Chris Cavallo. I was born on October 5, YR-16. I live in the Putnam Park Apartments. I was caught up in the fight that occurred at the intersection of Norton Road and Old State Pike in the parking lot of Fisher's Convenience Store on March 10, YR-1.

I was standing in front of Fisher's Convenience Store with some of the older guys from my neighborhood. They are Las Calaveras members, but I'm not part of all that. I play soccer with a few of the guys in the neighborhood league. Our team colors are red and white, so everyone always assumes I'm part of Las Calaveras gang, but I'm not. I am Italian, not Latino. I don't have a problem with those guys, and they don't have a problem with me.

We were just standing in the parking lot when four SUVs, or maybe three SUVs and one truck, pulled up real fast. Their tires screeched. A bunch of Stone Cross members—everyone calls them SC—piled out. There were maybe twenty of them. They came up fast and started yelling and pushing some of the guys in the parking lot. I backed up because this wasn't my fight.

The fighting started fast. Punches were flying, and I tried to turn and walk off. I got pushed from behind and fell to the ground. I don't know who pushed me. It took me a second to get my bearings. When I got to my knees, I looked over my right shoulder, and I saw this big SC with a baseball bat rushing towards me. I curled up in a little ball to protect myself. When no blow came, I looked to my right side, and I saw the SC with the bat struggling with B. B's real name is Victor Buentello. B had him from behind by his arms, but the guy still had the bat. There was this other guy on the ground next to me and right in front of the guy with the bat. They were only, at most, four feet away from me. The guy on the ground came up to a crouch and swung up with his right hand and hit the SC in the chest. The SC dropped the bat and crumbled to the ground. I saw the guy that hit the SC in the chest drop a knife. The SC was groaning loudly and holding his chest. I scrambled to my feet and took off.

Once things settled down a bit, maybe twenty minutes later, I came back to the scene to see what happened to the guy. I saw B standing in the crowd in the front yard across from the parking lot. I caught his eye, but there was a police officer talking to the people in the crowd. I don't know what the police officer was saying, but B slipped away before I had a chance to talk with him. I couldn't believe the SC was dead. The guy only stabbed him once, and it wasn't even a good shot. The guy with the knife swung kind of wild-like from a crouched position. The whole thing happened so fast. I don't know what happened to the knife or the bat.

The guy with the bat was a white man in his mid-twenties. He was big, maybe six feet tall and 250 pounds.

The guy with the knife lives in the neighborhood. I've seen him around. He is maybe twenty years old with black hair. He doesn't have an accent, but I think he is Latino. I've never seen him hang out with Las Calaveras members.

B is not a Las Calaveras member, but he hangs out with them sometimes at Sam and Taylor's Bodega and Pena's Sports Club. He also lives in the neighborhood. He is around twenty years old and Latino.

I have read this statement, and it is a true and accurate account of what I witnessed in the Fisher's Convenience Store parking lot on March 10, YR-1.

This statement was written and signed by the witness in the presence of Detective Terry Hefler.

Chris Cavallo

Chris Cavallo

March 10, YR-1

Date

STATEMENT OF MARTIN SALAS

My name is Martin Salas. I was born on May 8, YR-51. I have lived in the Putnam Park neighborhood for my entire fifty-one years. My address is 1144 Miller Lane. I live a few houses up from Ernesto Sanchez. I saw him running from a fight in the Fisher's Convenience Store parking lot on March 10, YR-1. I also know him from the neighborhood. He is a member of Las Calaveras.

On March 10, YR-1, I was walking to Fisher's Restaurant at approximately 3:00 p.m. I was alone. I left my house, walked south on Miller Lane, and turned right on Old State Pike. When I was about a half a block from the intersection of Norton Road and Old State Pike, I heard some loud voices. I couldn't understand what they were saying, but I could tell the people shouting were angry. I ran toward Fisher's Restaurant. Just a few weeks ago, a young girl in our neighborhood was killed in a drive-by shooting. The gangs in our neighborhood have really gotten out of hand. I ran toward the commotion to see if there were any innocent people in jeopardy.

When I got to the intersection of Norton Road and Old State Pike, I could see the fight across the intersection in the parking lot of Fisher's Convenience Store. Maybe forty kids were involved. About half of them were Las Calaveras members. I know that from their colors (red and white). They were in a fight with kids in black, probably Stone Cross. The Stone Cross is a new gang to the neighborhood. They have been feuding with Las Calaveras for the past year. Some of the kids in the fight had baseball bats, sticks, and pieces of two-by-four lumber. I crossed diagonally through the intersection of Norton Road and Old State Pike and started across the parking lot. Crowds of bystanders were forming in the front yard of the house across from Fisher's and at the edges of the parking lot.

I saw a few kids I recognized from my neighborhood. I only know one by name, Ernesto Sanchez. When I spotted Ernesto, he was on his knees. It was a pretty rough scene. Detective Hefler asked me if I saw anyone hitting Ernesto. I didn't see anyone specifically hit him, but there was so much going on. I was scanning the scene for my nephew, Paul Salas. He is my brother's sixteen-year-old son. I was focused on making sure he wasn't in the fight. By the time I scanned through the whole crowd, I caught a glimpse of Ernesto running across Old State Pike. The fight broke up as soon as the sirens could be heard.

I went into Fisher's Restaurant and ordered some pizza and a Coke. Luis Ambrose, the owner of Fisher's Restaurant, was talking about the fight. He kept walking in and out of the restaurant to follow what was happening in the parking lot. He came in and told us that one of the Stone Cross members was killed. After I finished my dinner, I left the restaurant and was stopped by Detective Hefler a few feet from the entrance of the restaurant. I told him what I saw. He asked me to come to the Nita City Police Department today and sign this statement.

I gave Detective Hefler Ernesto Sanchez's address at 1148 Miller Lane. I asked Detective Hefler not to mention my name in conjunction with this case because I was afraid for my safety and for my family's safety. I know Ernesto is in the Las Calaveras gang because my nephew Paul told me Neto, which is Ernesto's gang name, was a member of Las Calaveras. One afternoon when Ernesto was walking by the front of my house, a black SUV pulled up quickly behind him. Paul and I were about thirty feet away, watching from the porch. I jumped up because I was concerned for Ernesto's safety. Paul grabbed my arm and quickly said, "Don't worry, Neto's Las Calaveras, and that SUV belongs to Papa Ru." Everyone knows that Papa Ru is the head of Las Calaveras. This conversation happened about six months ago. I could not see into the SUV because the windows were tinted very dark. I don't know for sure who was inside the car. Ernesto seemed happy for the ride.

I have never witnessed Ernesto do anything illegal. However, when Ernesto was thirteen years old, I witnessed him beat up a younger boy, who was eleven years old. Ernesto was the aggressor in the fight. He punched the younger boy repeatedly in the face and stomach until the younger boy's father broke up the fight. The fight took place on the basketball courts in Putnam Park.

I have read this statement, and it is a true and accurate account of what I witnessed in the Fisher's Convenience Store parking lot on March 10, YR-1.

This statement was written and signed by the witness in the presence of Detective Terry Hefler.

[signature]

Martin Salas

March 11, YR-1

Date

Police Report, 3-13-YR-1, Ambrose Interview

State of Nita **Narrative Report** NPR 5490 (Rev. 07-YR-10) OPI D87				Page 1 of 2
Date of Incident/Occurrence 03-10-YR-1	Time 3:00 PM	NCIC Number 68474	Officer I.D. Number 2653	Number 000YR-1-056
"X" One ☐ Narrative ☒ Supplemental	"X" One ☒ Criminal report ☐ Other	Type Supplemental ("X" Applicable) ☐ Collision Update ☒ Fatal ☐ Hit and Run Update ☐ Hazardous materials ☐ School bus ☐ Other ______		
City/County/Judicial District Nita City/Darrow/First			Reporting District/Beat Putnam Park	Citation Number N/A
Location/Subject Fisher's Convenience Store, 679 Old State Pike			State Highway Related ☐ Yes ☒ No	

SUPPLEMENTAL NARRATIVE:

On March 11 and 12, YR-1, I visited Fisher's Restaurant at 679 Old State Pike, to interview Luis Ambrose. He was in the restaurant, but he was unable to speak with me because much of his staff quit after the stabbing. He was cooking and waiting tables. On March 13, YR-1, I was finally able to interview Mr. Ambrose at 7:30 a.m. He owns Fisher's Restaurant and is approximately fifty-five years old. I have talked to Mr. Ambrose on gang-related matters in the past. He is supportive of our anti-gang efforts and attends community meetings. He testified for the prosecution in two Las Calaveras prosecutions. Those Las Calaveras members were convicted in YR-2 of assault with a deadly weapon and possession with intent to distribute a schedule two controlled substance (cocaine). Mr. Ambrose has a reputation in the community and the police department for being straightforward and truthful.

I asked Mr. Ambrose if he witnessed any aspect of the March 10 fight. He told me that when he heard tires screech in the parking lot, he ran out of the main entrance of his restaurant and turned to the right. Fisher's Restaurant faces away from Old State Pike. The entrance to the restaurant is at the rear of the building, and you have to walk between the convenience store and restaurant to reach it. He said it was chaotic in the parking lot in front of the convenience store. About twenty Stone Cross members swarmed on about fifteen Las Calaveras. He identified the participants as gang members by their clothes—Las Calaveras in red and white and Stone Cross in black. He said he saw a few kids that are not Las Calaveras members get caught up in the fight. He saw a kid named Ernesto Sanchez and another named Victor Buentello, who are not gang members, standing with the Las Calaveras members. He calls Ernesto Sanchez "Neto." He saw Neto get punched in the face. He ran to the door of his restaurant and called in for someone to call the police. He ran back to the exterior corner of his restaurant and saw Neto in a squatting position with Victor holding a guy with a bat off Neto. Mr. Ambrose was not sure if the guy with the bat was the guy who punched Neto in the face. Mr. Ambrose turned back to the door of his restaurant to tell the waitress in the doorway to call the police again. By the time he turned back to the fight, Neto and Victor were running away, the guy with the bat was on the ground, and police sirens could be heard.

Mr. Ambrose confirmed that the guy that was killed was the guy with the bat. Mr. Ambrose never saw a knife in Neto's hand and was surprised that he would carry a weapon.

Mr. Ambrose knows Neto and Victor. Neto is a student at Nita Community College and often does his homework in the restaurant. He says that neither Neto nor Victor wear Las Calaveras colors. He knows Victor because he dated Victor's mother Lily from June YR-2 to January YR-1. The relationship ended because Lily reconciled with her husband, Carlos. Mr. Ambrose is still friends with Lily. Victor lives at 210 Ashby Court. He doesn't know Neto's address.

Mr. Ambrose's restaurant was vandalized with Stone Cross graffiti numerous times in the past month.

Preparer's Name, Rank, Division, and I.D. Number	Date
Hefler, Terry, Detective, Street Enforcement Unit, 2653	***03-13-YR-1***

YR-10 654613

Exhibit 7 (con't.)

Police Report, 3-13-YR-1, Ambrose Interview

STATE OF NITA **NARRATIVE REPORT** NPR 5490 (Rev. 07-YR-10) OPI D87				Page 2 of 2
Date of Incident/Occurrence 03-10-YR-1	Time 3:00 PM	NCIC Number 68474	Officer I.D. Number 2653	Number 000YR-1-056
"X" One ☐ Narrative ☒ Supplemental	"X" One ☒ Criminal report ☐ Other	Type Supplemental ("X" Applicable) ☐ Collision Update ☒ Fatal ☐ Hit and Run Update ☐ Hazardous materials ☐ School bus☐ Other ______		
City/County/Judicial District Nita City/Darrow/First			Reporting District/Beat Putnam Park	Citation Number N/A
Location/Subject Fisher's Convenience Store, 679 Old State Pike			State Highway Related ☐ Yes ☒ No	

SUPPLEMENTAL NARRATIVE:

After interviewing Mr. Ambrose on March 13, YR-1, I photographed the Fisher's Convenience Store parking lot from various angles. The photographs are attached.

At approximately 3:40 p.m. on that same day, I arrived at 210 Ashby Court to talk to Victor Buentello. I asked him to come to the police station to talk to me about his participation in the fight on March 10, YR-1. I clearly told Mr. Buentello that he had a right to refuse my request and that he was not under arrest. Mr. Buentello agreed to accompany me to the station. Before we left for the station, I asked for Mr. Buentello's consent to search his residence. He denied my request to search.

Mr. Buentello provided me with a written statement at the police station. His complete written statement is attached.

Preparer's Name, Rank, Division, and I.D. Number	Date
Hefler, Terry, Detective, Street Enforcement Unit, 2653	***03-13-YR-1***

YR-10 654613

Exhibit 8

Photo of Fisher's (1)

Exhibit 9

Photo of Fisher's (2)

03-13-YR-1 Report Supplemental, Detective Terry Hefler

Exhibit 10

Photo of Fisher's (3)

STATEMENT OF VICTOR BUENTELLO

My name Is Victor Buentello. I was born May 4, YR-21, and I am a Hispanic American. Both of my parents are originally from Mexico. I voluntarily came to the police station to talk to the police about the fight in the Fisher's Convenience Store parking lot on March 10, YR-1. I know I am not under arrest and that I am free to leave at any time. I know that I do not have to answer the police officer's questions and can stop the interview at any time. I want to tell the police what happened, because I don't want Neto to get in trouble. He was just defending himself.

I live at 210 Ashby Court, Nita City, Nita. I live with my parents. We have lived in this neighborhood all my life.

On March 10, YR-1, I went to Putnam Park with Neto to play basketball. Neto's first name is Ernesto, but everyone just calls him Neto for short. I used to date his sister, Marta. I walked over to Neto's house, 1148 Miller Lane, at about 11:40 a.m. On the way to the park from his house, Neto told me he had heard that Stone Cross was planning an attack on Las Calaveras this weekend. He said he was surprised nothing bad had happened on Friday or Saturday night. He said he thought something bad would happen soon. Neto was saying how much he hates gangs, especially Stone Cross, because of what they did to that little girl a few weeks back. I think Neto knew her. She was shot in a drive-by. Everybody hates Stone Cross for it. We also talked about how Marta was getting more involved with Las Calaveras. Neto seemed worried about her. We got to the park at approximately noon. The courts are on the far side of the park from our neighborhood. When we got there, the games had already started. We have been playing at the park with the same group of guys for years. We all used to play soccer together when we were in elementary and middle school. Most of the guys still live in the neighborhood.

I was wearing an old red sweatshirt and dark grey sweatpants. I tried to find the sweatshirt for Detective Hefler, but I couldn't find it in my house. My friends are always borrowing my clothes. I refused to let the cops search my house because the house belongs to my parents, and it wouldn't be right to give the cops permission to go through my parents' belongings.

On that day, we played basketball for about three hours. Neto quit playing, and when he left, everyone just stopped playing. I left with "Flaco." I don't know his real name, but he plays on my soccer team. He has only been playing with the team for a few months. He is new to the neighborhood. I don't know where he lives. When we left the basketball court, we were only thirty yards, at most, behind Neto. We called out to him to wait, but he didn't respond. I don't think he heard us. We walked across the park to Norton Road and crossed over First Street.

When I got to the intersection of Norton Road and Old State Pike, we could see a group of Las Calaveras members hanging around in the parking lot in front of Fisher's Convenience Store. There were maybe twenty members there. I was surprised to see Neto heading right for them, especially after what he had said to me earlier that morning about the possibility of a fight with SC. He usually steers clear of that crowd. I know a lot of them from my soccer team, through

Neto's sister, and because they hang out at my favorite restaurant—Herrera's Latin Cuisine. I've been seeing this girl; her name is Ann Wilson. She hangs out with them, too. I'm not really into the whole gang thing. I have lots of friends from lots of different crowds.

As we approached the intersection of Norton Road and Old State Pike, I could see that Ann was about thirty feet from the group of guys. She was leaning against the front of Fisher's Convenience Store. Flaco and I started heading in her direction.

I lost track of Neto for a minute because he was in the middle of the group. I was about halfway across the parking lot when the Stone Cross members showed up. Everybody calls the gang "SC," and members are "SCers." I heard the SUVs' tires squeal when they stopped. I started walking over to the group to get Neto out of there. He isn't much of a fighter. He's a college guy. By the time I got there, the SCers were already throwing punches. I saw a big guy with a bat standing over Neto, who was on his knees. I shouted at Neto to "watch out." The guy with the bat swung it over his shoulder and hit Neto's arm. Neto had put his arm over his head. The guy was swinging the bat back to take another crack at Neto. I ran up and grabbed the guy's arms. I lifted his arms in the air. He had both hands on the bat. Right at that moment, Neto moved to a crouching position and swung his right arm up and out. He hit the guy in the chest with a knife. It wasn't a big knife, but when it struck the guy in the chest he fell to the ground. He went limp. I didn't know what happened at first. It happened so quickly. The guy was on the ground moaning and holding his chest. Neto jumped up and dropped the knife. That was actually the first time I saw the knife. I didn't really see it go into the guy's chest because my view was partially blocked—I was standing a bit behind the guy. Not completely behind him but enough behind him that I couldn't see his chest. I was to the guy's left. I made a diagram of where everyone was for Detective Hefler.

We ran. I don't know what happened to Flaco or Ann. Neto ran toward his house. I stopped running when I crossed Old State Pike. I stood with a crowd of bystanders in the front yard of the house across the street. About ten seconds later, I could hear the sirens from the cop cars. They got there about a minute or two later. As soon as the gangs heard the sirens, the SC guys jumped in the cars, and the Las Calaveras ran. They all just left the guy lying there. He wasn't moaning anymore. He was just lying there. I think he was already dead. A cop rolled him over and checked his pulse. The ambulance got there about two minutes later. They put a sheet over the guy, so I guess he was dead.

The dead guy was a large white guy, mid-twenties, with dark brown/black hair. He was at least six feet. I'm only five-foot-ten-inches tall. He definitely had a few inches on me. He was about 250 pounds. I'm about 200 pounds, but I'm in good shape. This guy was thick around the middle.

I walked home and stayed there until the next night. There were cops everywhere. They were going door to door. I didn't answer the door when they knocked. The day after the fight, at around 7:00 p.m., I went over to Neto's house to see how he was doing. I told Neto what I saw. He told me what he remembered from the fight. He was really freaked out that he had killed the guy with one swing. I think it was just sinking in that he had killed the guy. He really was just protecting himself, and I was just trying to protect him. I can't believe he is in trouble for protecting himself.

I know that Neto always carries a knife. I don't think he has ever pulled it on anyone. Or at least I never saw him use it.

I didn't talk to the police before today because I didn't want Neto to get in trouble. I am not a member of Las Calaveras.

I have read this statement, and it is a true and accurate account of what happened in the parking lot of Fisher's Convenience Store on March 10, YR-1.

This statement was written and signed by the witness in the presence of Detective Terry Hefler.

Victor Buentello

Victor Buentello

March 13, YR-1

Date

Exhibit 11

Buentello Diagram of Crime Scene

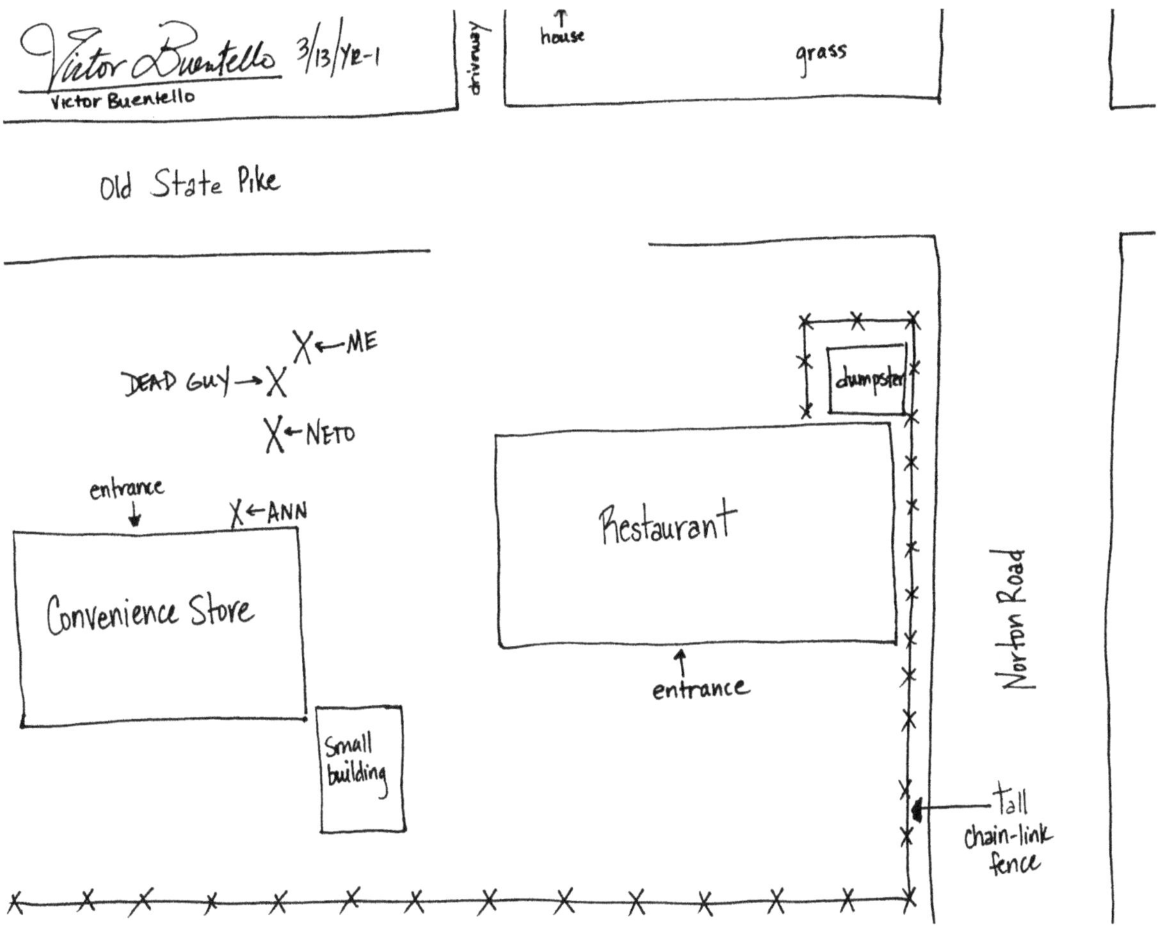

(hand drawn by Buentello)

Exhibit 12

Buentello FBI Criminal Activity Record

UNITED STATES
DEPARTMENT OF JUSTICE
WASHINGTON, DC

Federal Bureau of Investigation

CRIMINAL ACTIVITY RECORD 10/30/YR-1

The following FBI record, NUMBER 523-899-T4, is furnished for OFFICIAL USE ONLY. Information shown on this identification record represents data furnished to the FBI by fingerprint contributors.

Subject: Victor G. Buentello
Date of Birth: 5/4/YR-21
Id. No.: 4-3167-594

Contributor of Record Information	Name	Arrested or Received	Charge	Disposition
PD Nita City, Nita	Victor G. Buentello	5/2/YR-3	Misdemeanor Petit Larceny/ Vandalism	Found Guilty Fined $500
PD Nita City, Nita	Victor G. Buentello	6/23/YR-2	Misdemeanor Assault	Found Guilty Sentenced 30 days suspended
PD Nita City, Nita	Victor G. Buentello	7/28/YR-1	Felony Forgery	Found Guilty Sentenced 60 days w/30 days suspended

Exhibit 13

BUENTELLO CERTIFIED CRIMINAL CONVICTIONS

CRIMINAL COURT RECORD

NITA STATE FELONIES & MISDEMEANORS

	BUENTELLO, VICTOR G.
SSN:	**324-79-8805**
Date of Birth:	**May 4, YR-21**
Order #:	**4046207-1**
Request Date:	**10/29/YR-1**

SOURCE: NITA STATE PATROL

Source Records Reviewed: **From YR-4 to present**

Search Criteria: **DOB and ARRESTING AGENCY and OFFENSE DATE**

Name is listed as:
BUENTELLO, VICTOR G.
BUENTELLO, VIC
BUENTELLO, "B"

Physical description in court records:

SEX: M   RACE: H   HGT: 5′10″   WGT: 200   EYE: BRO   HAIR: BLA

Case No: **DYR-1CR027385**
Arresting Agency: **NITA CITY POLICE DEPARTMENT**
File Date: **08/02/YR-3**
Arrest Date: **05/02/YR-3**
Offense Date: **04/28/YR-3**
Offense: **MISDEMEANOR – PETIT LARCENY**
VANDALISM
Disposition Date: **08/01/YR-3**
Disposition: **FOUND GUILTY BY JUDGE;**
$500;
COURT COSTS

Additional Info: **SCARS/MARKS: N/A**

Date: 4/1/YR-1

Attested: *Richard Poplar*

Clerk, Nita City Circuit Court

Exhibit 14

Buentello Certified Criminal Convictions

CRIMINAL COURT RECORD
NITA STATE FELONIES & MISDEMEANORS

	BUENTELLO, VICTOR G.
SSN:	324-79-8805
Date of Birth:	May 4, YR-21
Order #:	4046207-2
Request Date:	10/29/YR-1

SOURCE: NITA STATE PATROL

Source Records Reviewed: From YR-4 to present
Search Criteria: DOB and ARRESTING AGENCY and OFFENSE DATE

Name is listed as: BUENTELLO, VICTOR G.
BUENTELLO, VIC
BUENTELLO, "B"

Physical description in court records:
SEX: M RACE: H HGT: 5'10" WGT: 200 EYE: BRO HAIR: BLA

Case No: DYR-1CR027385
Arresting Agency: NITA CITY POLICE DEPARTMENT
File Date: 09/13/YR-2
Arrest Date: 06/23/YR-2
Offense Date: 06/23/YR-2
Offense: MISDEMEANOR – ASSAULT
Disposition Date: 09/12/YR-3
Disposition: FOUND GUILTY BY JUDGE;
30 DAYS JAIL; SENTENCE SUSPENDED;
COURT COSTS

Additional Info: SCARS/MARKS: N/A

Date: 4/1/YR-1

Attested: *Richard Poplar*

Clerk, Nita City Circuit Court

Exhibit 15

BUENTELLO CERTIFIED CRIMINAL CONVICTIONS

CRIMINAL COURT RECORD
NITA STATE FELONIES & MISDEMEANORS

	BUENTELLO, VICTOR G.
SSN:	324-79-8805
Date of Birth:	May 4, YR-21
Order #:	4046207-3
Request Date:	10/29/YR-1

SOURCE: NITA STATE PATROL

Source Records Reviewed: From YR-4 to present
Search Criteria: DOB and ARRESTING AGENCY and OFFENSE DATE

Name is listed as: BUENTELLO, VICTOR G.
BUENTELLO, VIC
BUENTELLO, "B"

Physical description in court records:
SEX: M RACE: H HGT: 5′10″ WGT: 200 EYE: BRO HAIR: BLA

Case No: DYR-1CR027385
Arresting Agency: NITA CITY POLICE DEPARTMENT
File Date: 08/29/YR-1
Arrest Date: 07/28/YR-1
Offense Date: 07/21/YR-1
Offense: FELONY – FORGERY
Disposition Date: 08/28/YR-1
Disposition: GUILTY PLEA;
60 DAYS PRISON; 30 DAYS SUSPENDED;
30 DAYS CREDIT FOR TIME SERVED;
COURT COSTS

Additional Info: SCARS/MARKS: N/A

Date: 4/1/YR-1

Attested: *Richard Poplar*

Clerk, Nita City Circuit Court

Exhibit 16

Police Report, 3-14-YR-1

State of Nita **Narrative Report** NPR 5490 (Rev. 07-YR-10) OPI D87				Page 1 of 1
Date of Incident/Occurrence 03-10-YR-1	Time 3:00 PM	NCIC Number 68474	Officer I.D. Number 2653	Number 000YR-1-056
"X" One ☐ Narrative ☒ Supplemental	"X" One ☒ Criminal report ☐ Other	Type Supplemental ("X" Applicable) ☐ Collision Update ☒ Fatal ☐ Hit and Run Update ☐ Hazardous materials ☐ School bus☐ Other ______		
City/County/Judicial District Nita City/Darrow/First			Reporting District/Beat Putnam Park	Citation Number N/A
Location/Subject Fisher's Convenience Store, 679 Old State Pike			State Highway Related ☐ Yes ☒ No	

SUPPLEMENTAL NARRATIVE:

At approximately 10:30 a.m., I arrived at 1148 Miller Lane to execute an arrest warrant on Ernesto Sanchez. Mr. Sanchez opened the door when I knocked. I placed him under arrest without incident. He consented to a search of his premises. I searched the premises for clothing and other items consistent with Las Calaveras gang membership. I located a red and white ice hockey jersey in the clothes dryer. I photographed the jersey and placed it in an evidence bag with my initials on the label. I placed the evidence bag in the evidence locker in the trunk of my vehicle and later stored it in the evidence room at the Nita City Police Department. The photograph is attached. I also found two skull sketches on the dresser in the bedroom that Mr. Sanchez identified as his bedroom. The sketches are attached.

At my request, Mr. Sanchez surrendered his cellphone. Upon searching his phone, I found no calls or texts with any known gang members.

I read Mr. Sanchez his *Miranda* warnings and he waived those warnings. His written rights waiver is attached. Mr. Sanchez identified the jersey as the shirt he was wearing during the fight on March 10, YR-1, in the parking lot in front of Fisher's Convenience Store. He confessed to stabbing the victim and identified the butterfly knife found at the scene as the knife he used in the stabbing. His complete written statement is attached.

Preparer's Name, Rank, Division, and I.D. Number	Date
Hefler, Terry, Detective, Street Enforcement Unit, 2653	***03-14-YR-1***

YR-10 654613

Exhibit 17

RIGHTS WAIVER FORM

RIGHTS WAIVER

POLICE DEPARTMENT

CASE NO.	DATE	TIME	PLACE
000YR-1-056	03/14/YR-1	11:24 A.M.	NITA CITY POLICE DEPARTMENT

You, Ernesto Sanchez, are now being questioned about the crime of murder and gang participation. Detective Hefler has been identified to you as a member of the Nita City Police Department. Before questioning begins, it is required that you be advised of your rights under the law, and that you understand these rights.

1. You have the right to remain silent.
2. Anything you say can be used against you in court.
3. You have the right to talk to a lawyer before we ask you any questions and to have a lawyer with you during questioning.
4. If you cannot afford a lawyer, and want one, one will be provided for you by the court.
5. If you decide to answer questions now, without a lawyer present, you still have the right to stop answering questions at any time.

WAIVER OF RIGHTS

I have read this statement of my rights and I understand what my rights are. I am willing to make a statement and answer questions. No threats, promises, or offers of reward have been made to me.

SIGNATURE

WITNESS		
SGT. MICHAEL WHITE		
DATE	*TIME*	*PLACE*
03/14/YR-1	*11:24 A.M.*	*NITA CITY POLICE DEPARTMENT*

Statement of Ernesto Sanchez

My name is Ernesto Sanchez. I was born November 5, YR-21. I am Latino, five-foot-ten-inches tall, and weigh about 195 pounds. I have been advised of my rights and waive my right to remain silent and have an attorney present when I am questioned. I give this statement freely and voluntarily. I want to tell the police what happened on March 10, YR-1.

I live at 1148 Miller Lane, Nita City, Nita. I have lived there with my parents and sister all my life.

On March 10, YR-1, I went to Putnam Park to shoot some hoops. I walked to the park from my house. It is about a mile walk. I got to the park at approximately noon. The basketball courts are in the southwest corner of the park, and when I got there, people were already playing pickup games. The same group of guys plays basketball at these courts every Sunday afternoon. We've played here for years. Some of us played soccer together when we were kids. Most of the guys still live in the neighborhood. I walked to the courts with Victor Buentello. Everyone calls him "B." I've known B since we were kids, but we have never been close friends. For a short time, maybe three months, my younger sister, Marta, dated B. She broke up with him when she started dating her current boyfriend. I would say B dated Marta from July to November, YR-2.

On March 10, YR-1, I was wearing a red and white ice hockey jersey. Detective Hefler has the jersey. I was wearing black sweatpants. On the way to the park, I was wearing a black, hooded sweatshirt with a zipper up the front and front pockets. I took the sweatshirt off when I started playing basketball.

B was wearing a faded red sweatshirt and dark grey sweatpants. Since we were both wearing dark clothes, we played on the same team.

We played basketball for something like three hours. I was hungry, so I headed to Fisher's Restaurant. The restaurant is located at the intersection of Norton Road and Old State Pike. It is on my way home from the park.

I left the basketball court alone, but I learned later that B and some kid I only know as "Flaco" left the courts behind me. I had earphones in, listening to music, so I didn't hear them call after me. I walked up Norton Road and over the First Street overpass. I had to walk past Fisher's Restaurant on my left because it is surrounded by a high fence. You enter the parking lot for Fisher's Convenience Store and Restaurant from Old State Pike. When I got to the intersection of Norton Road and Old State Pike, I looked to my left and saw a group of people gathered in the parking lot in front of Fisher's Convenience Store. There were about fifteen guys there. I had to walk past them to get to the entrance of Fisher's Restaurant. When I got about fifty feet away from the group, I recognized some of the guys. They were Las Calaveras gang members. Some of them went to high school with Marta. There were also some older guys there, guys my age. I recognized a few of them from the neighborhood. I said "Hey," and a few said "Hey" back. I don't hang out with that crowd. They are pretty rough, but I don't mess with them, and they don't mess with me. I know my little sister hangs out with them. She met them when she was dating B. I think B plays on their soccer team. I'm not saying he is a gang member, he just knows them pretty well. The colors of the soccer team are red and white. Las Calaveras all wear red and white warm-up suits. The rumor is that the gang started as a soccer team, but now most of the members don't even play soccer, and they are all involved in criminal activity. They sell drugs in the neighborhood.

One guy waved me over. I took my headphones off. He called me "Neto." I don't know his real name. Everyone calls him "Papa Ru." He is the head guy. I always see him bossing everyone around. I walked over to see what he wanted. It surprised me that he knew me by name because we had never spoken to each other before that day. I got to within about five feet of him when all of a sudden some SUVs and a truck pulled up. A bunch of guys and some girls got out and walked up to the Las Calaveras group. It was clear they were angry. I wasn't going to stick around to hear why. I knew they were Stone Cross, or SC as everyone calls them, because they were all wearing black. They are always coming to our neighborhood and starting fights. About a month ago, there was a drive-by shooting two blocks from my house. A young girl was killed. She was the little sister of Jesse Lopez, a close friend of mine. Everyone knows SC was responsible.

I turned to walk away, and some large SC guy (white, mid-twenties, dark brown hair) pushed me back against some teenager in our group. The fighting broke out quick. I couldn't get away. I turned around, and the big guy hit me on the right side of my face with his fist and in the stomach. I went down to my knees. I looked up just in time to put up my left arm and block a baseball bat that was coming toward my head. I dropped my sweatshirt from my left hand when the bat hit my left arm. I had a big welt and bruise, but it has faded since the fight. I heard B say, "Neto, watch out," right as I was blocking the baseball bat. B tried to grab the bat from the guy. I don't know where B came from. He must have been walking behind me the whole time. I scrambled for my sweatshirt and grabbed my butterfly knife from the pocket. I flicked out the blade with my right hand and swung upward wildly. I thought maybe I would catch the guy's hand and he would drop the bat. I was just trying to get the guy off me. On my first swing, I hit the guy who had the bat in the chest. It is not a big knife, but it went in all the way. I freaked out. I dropped the knife and ran. I don't know what happened to the knife, the bat, or my sweatshirt. The big guy was lying on the ground when I ran. He was alive when I left, because I could hear him groaning.

I cut through the yard across the street and ran straight home. I put some ice on my jaw and the welt on my left arm from where he hit me with the bat. I changed out of my red hockey jersey because I didn't want anyone to think I was Las Calaveras. I went back out to see what was going on. That's when a news reporter stopped by and asked if I saw what happened. I told her she could interview me as long as they didn't show my face. I didn't want my face all over the place talking about what happened. You know, the gangs don't really like you talking about them. They especially don't like you running your mouth if you aren't even in the gang. That's why I didn't want my face shown. The reporter asked what I knew about the two gangs. I showed her the Las Calaveras gang sign. I mean, I didn't think it was a big deal because everyone around the neighborhood already has seen it at one point or another. I said I wasn't at the fight because I was scared I was going to get in trouble.

I couldn't believe it when she said the guy died. I was just protecting myself. I didn't go to the police because I didn't want to get in trouble. I only have a few more classes to take at Nita Community College before I receive my associate's degree in business administration. With that degree, I can get a good job and move out of this neighborhood. I want to get my family out of this place.

Detective Hefler searched my house the morning of March 14, YR-1. He found the red and white jersey I wore on March 10. He also found some of my Day of the Dead drawings in my bedroom. I like to draw, and I am Mexican, so the skulls are common in my house. My mom has a few skull figurines, and she isn't a gang member. There were also drawings I made of animals and plants in my bedroom. I don't know if he photographed them.

Detective Hefler arrested me on March 14, YR-1. He showed me copies of two Flashgrams I sent from my Flash account on March 10. I told him they were mine. I also showed Detective Hefler the bruise I still had on my left arm. He photographed it. I identified my knife. I know it is my knife because it has a drop of red paint on the handle. I found it in Putnam Park about three years ago. I always carry that knife for protection. My neighborhood is not a safe place. I've only had to pull it out twice before March 10. I've never touched anyone with it before March 10. I only showed it to get guys to leave me alone. It has been about a year since the last time I pulled it out. It is not illegal to carry it, because the blade is only four inches long. I checked the law on that before I started carrying it.

Detective Hefler also asked me about my Heart 24/7 account and presented me with a warrant to take screenshots of the tracking data on my phone. I gave him my phone and he took screenshots from my account for the months of February and March of Y-1. After he looked at the screenshots of my account, he showed them to me and asked if the Heart 24/7 app had accurately captured my movements on Friday evenings. I told him it accurately tracked my movements. I explained to him that I go out with my friends every Friday and that all the places that showed up on Heart 24/7 were my friends' houses, local restaurants, or parks. I also told him that those friends were not gang members, and I specifically pointed out that the address on Sargent Lane was my friend Flaco's. Detective Hefler said that the locations were "gang meetings." I don't know anything about "gang meetings" and I was not meeting with gang members at any of those locations.

I am not a member of Las Calaveras. I've never even been arrested before.

I have read this statement, and it is a true and accurate account of what happened in the parking lot of Fisher's Convenience Store on March 10, YR-1.

This statement was written and signed by the witness in the presence of Detective Terry Hefler.

Ernesto Sanchez [signature]

Ernesto Sanchez

March 14, YR-1

Date

Exhibit 18

Photo of Bruise (1)

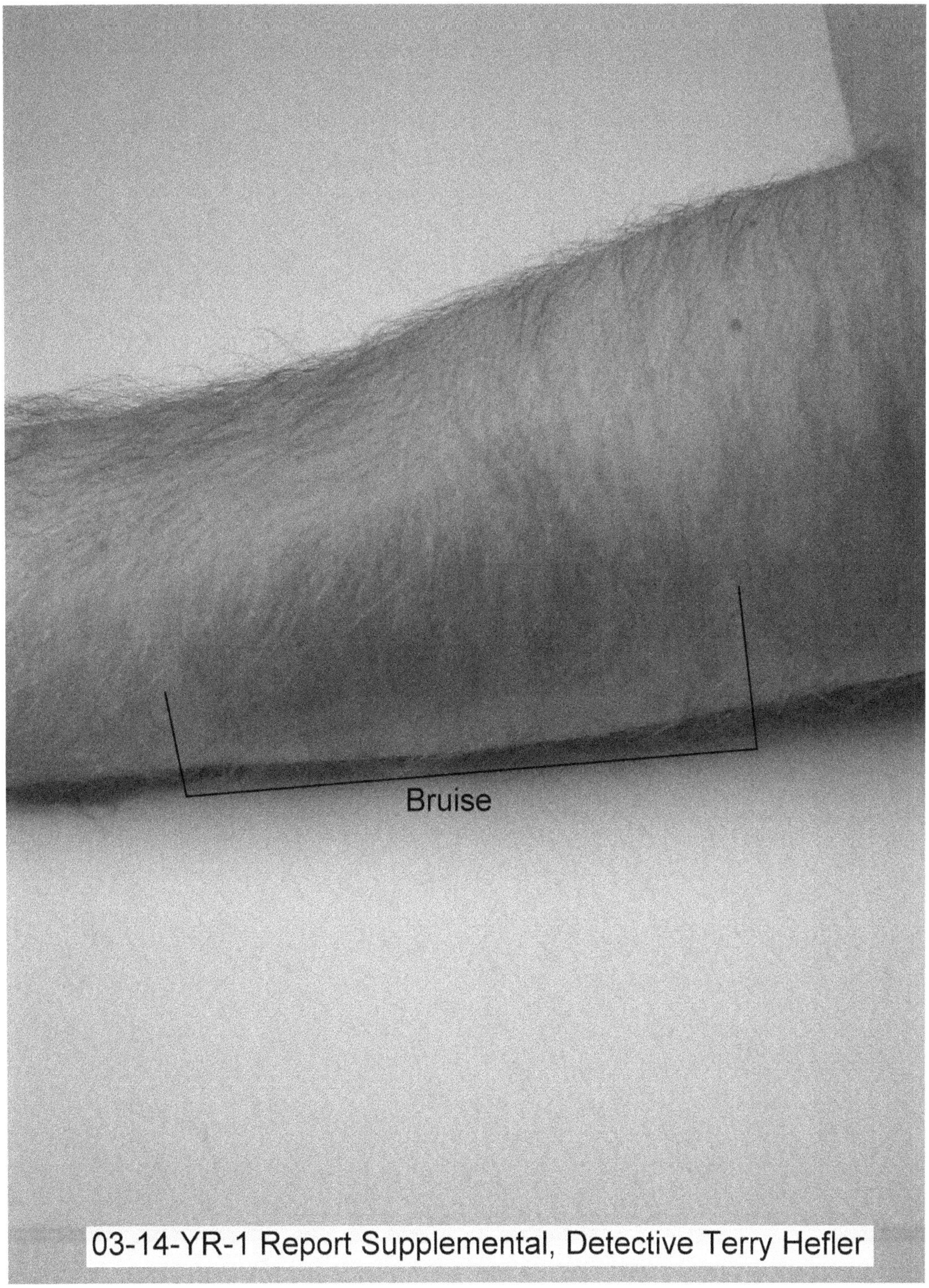

Exhibit 19

Photo of Bruise (2)

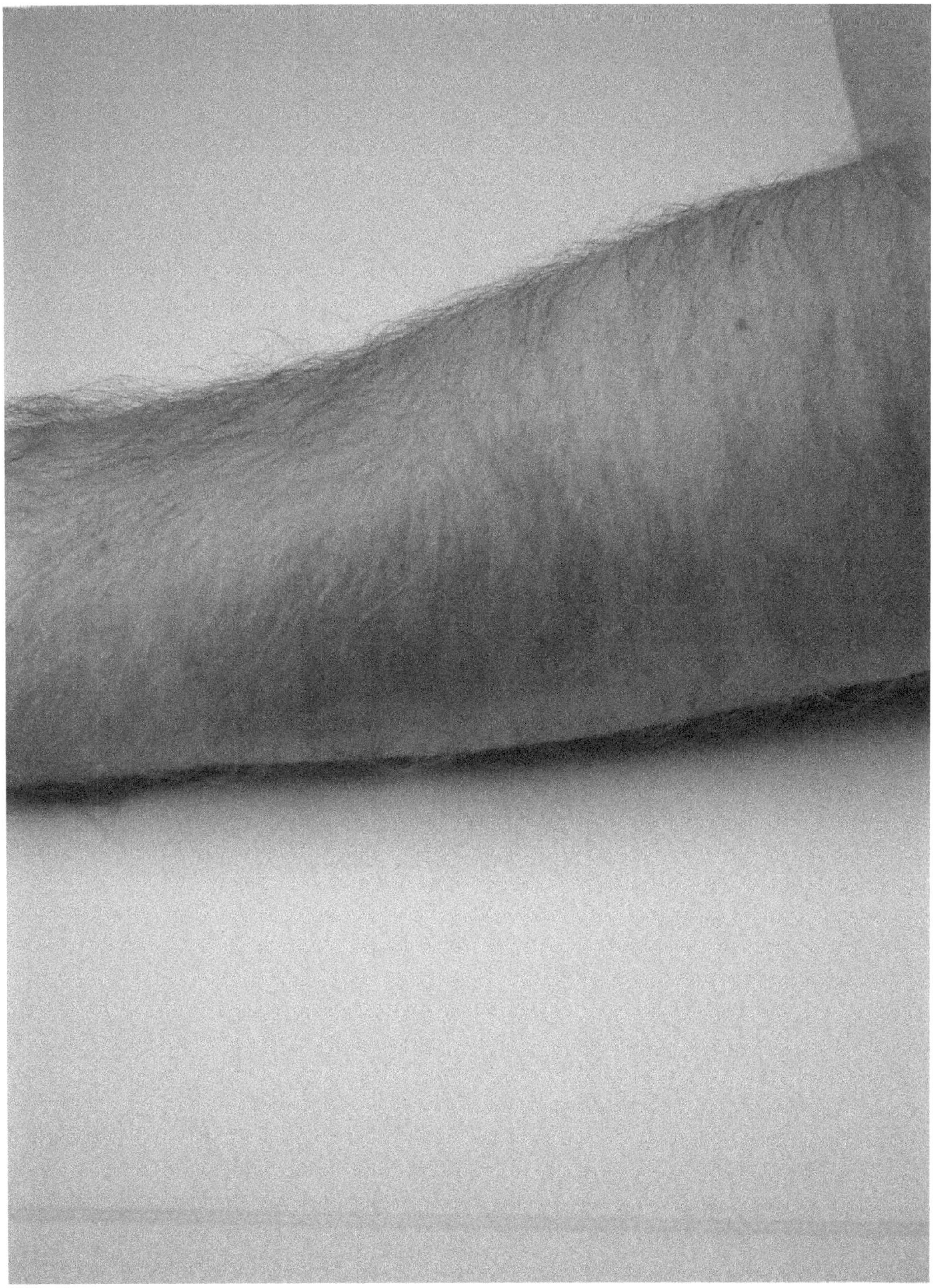

Exhibit 20

Photo of Hockey Jersey (1)

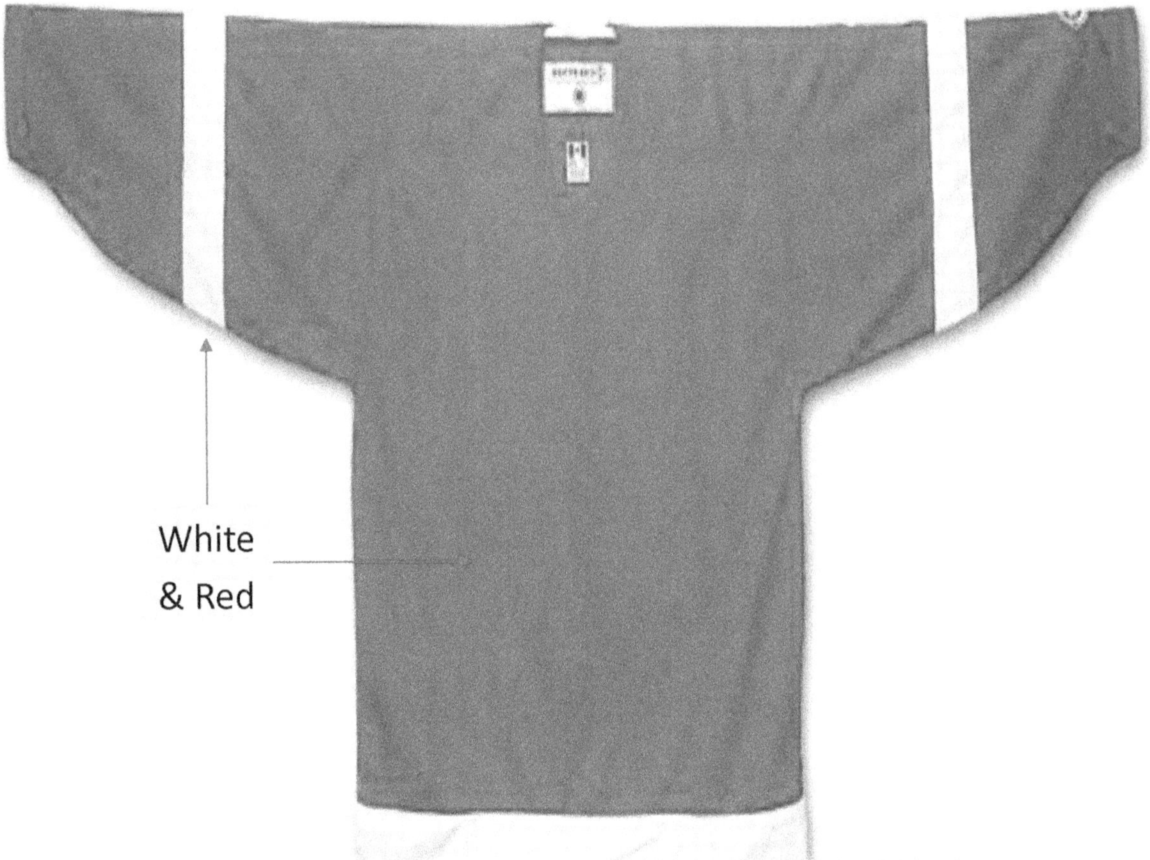

03-14-YR-1 Report Supplemental, Detective Terry Hefler

Exhibit 21

PHOTO OF HOCKEY JERSEY (2)

Exhibit 22

Skull Sketch (1)

Exhibit 23

Skull Sketch (2)

Exhibit 24

News Interview Transcript (Digital recording at http://bit.ly/1P20Jea) (Password: Sanchez3)

Transcript: Interview with Ernesto Sanchez

Date: March 10, YR-1

Time: 3:39 pm

Reporter: This is Gloria Rodriguez reporting from outside the Fisher's Convenience Store, where yet another gang fight has taken place. We're told that about thirty minutes ago a man was stabbed, and he is now dead. We're here with Mr. Sanchez, but Mr. Sanchez has asked to keep his face off camera. Mr. Sanchez, what happened?

Ernesto Sanchez: Well, look, I wasn't there but I heard that there were about thirty to forty guys from Las Calaveras and Stone Cross Gang, and they all got into this big fight.

Reporter: How do you know that those gangs were involved?

Ernesto Sanchez: Well, one of my friends told me. But, you know everyone knows that Las Calaveras wears red and white and Stone Cross Gang wears all black. Uh, Stone Cross usually has a tattoo of a Celtic cross and Las Calaveras has a stone, uh, skull tattoo all over their bodies.

Reporter: What else do you know about gangs?

Ernesto Sanchez: Look, I mean, I dunno much, uh, but I do know that Stone Cross thinks they run Nita City but it's really Las Calaveras that runs it. You know they have this gang sign and everyone knows and respects it.

Reporter: Would you mind showing us what that gang sign is?

Ernesto Sanchez: Yeah; it's this [flashes gang sign]. You got the "L" and the "C."

Reporter: Thank you, Mr. Sanchez. This is Gloria Rodriguez signing off.

Exhibit 25

Sanchez Flashgram Message 1

Neto Sanchez @putnamparkneto • 3:42PM - 10 Mar YR-1

Lucky I had my knife. #closecall

Exhibit 26

Sanchez Flashgram Message 2

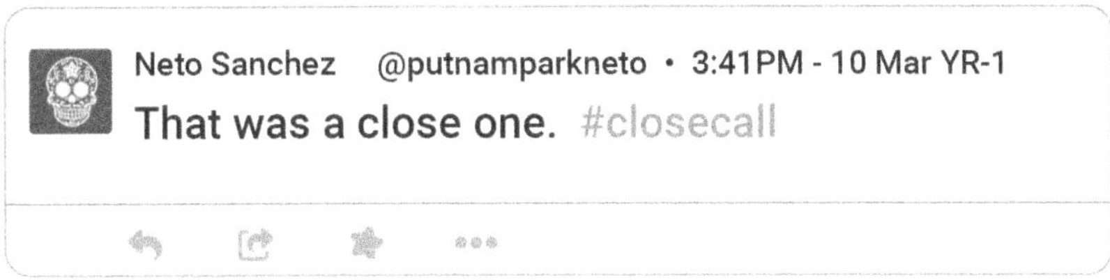

Neto Sanchez @putnamparkneto • 3:41PM - 10 Mar YR-1

That was a close one. #closecall

Exhibit 27

Police Report, 3-16-YR-1, Photo Identification

State of Nita **Narrative Report** **NPR 5490 (Rev. 07-YR-10) OPI D87**				**Page 1 of 1**
Date of Incident/Occurrence 03-10-YR-1	Time 3:00 PM	NCIC Number 68474	Officer I.D. Number 2653	Number 000YR-1-056
"X" One ☐ Narrative ☒ Supplemental	"X" One ☒ Criminal report ☐ Other	Type Supplemental ("X" Applicable) ☐ Collision Update ☐ Hazardous materials	☒ Fatal ☐ School bus	☐ Hit and Run Update ☐ Other ______
City/County/Judicial District Nita City/Darrow/First			Reporting District/Beat Putnam Park	Citation Number N/A
Location/Subject Fisher's Convenience Store, 679 Old State Pike			State Highway Related ☐ Yes ☒ No	

SUPPLEMENTAL NARRATIVE:

I met with Mary Kelly today, March 16, YR-1. I met with her at her residence to show her a photo spread of ten young Latino males who roughly fit the physical description of the stabber that she provided. The photographs were all of a similar size and format. The photographs were acquired from booking photographs and photographs used in other investigations.

I asked Ms. Kelly to review the stack one photograph at a time and to select the photograph, if any, that she recognized as the man who stabbed the victim on March 10, YR-1. I reassured her that she did not need to select a photograph if she did not recognize any of photographs as that of the stabber. She went through the entire stack of photographs one at a time and selected one photograph. She positively identified the photograph of Ernesto Sanchez as the young man she saw involved in the stabbing of March 10, YR-1. Ms. Kelly identified Ernesto Sanchez as "the guy who stabbed the victim." She wrote that phrase on the back of the photograph.

Preparer's Name, Rank, Division, and I.D. Number	Date
Hefler, Terry, Detective, Street Enforcement Unit, 2653	***03-16-YR-1***

YR-10 654613

Exhibit 28

Autopsy Report

NITA CITY CORONER'S OFFICE AUTOPSY REPORT

Case Title: In re Connor, Nita City Police Department

Pathologist: Lee Taylor, MD

Autopsy No.: 19845

Physician: Deputy County Coroner, Nita City, Nita

Patient: Connor, Patrick J.

Age: 24

Sex: M

Race: Caucasian

Date, Hour of Death: 3/10/YR-1, 3:10 p.m.

Date, Hour Autopsy: 3/10/YR-1, 11:00 p.m.

CLINICAL DATA

On March 10, YR-1, at 3:28 p.m., Detective Terry Hefler summoned the coroner's office to 680 Old State Pike to obtain the body of the deceased, Patrick J. Connor, for an autopsy. As the deputy coroner of the Nita City Coroner's Office, I met Detective Hefler in the parking lot in front of Fisher's Convenience Store at the intersection of Old State Pike and Norton Road and retrieved the body. The deceased was on his back on the pavement, approximately fifty feet from the front of the convenience store. At 4:20 p.m., the body was tagged and transferred to the Nita City morgue.

The postmortem examination began at 11:00 p.m. on March 10, YR-1. I took X-rays consisting of lateral torso, front and back of the chest, and flat plate of the abdomen prior to the autopsy. I labeled each X-ray with the date, autopsy number, and the letters "PJC." No retained foreign bodies were noted.

Detective Terry Hefler of the Nita City Police Department was present throughout the postmortem examination.

DIAGNOSIS

Stab wound to left anterior thorax.

Exhibit 28 (cont.)

Autopsy Report

CAUSE OF DEATH

Massive left hemothorax secondary to exsanguination from laceration of the left ventricular wall.

GENERAL EXTERNAL APPEARANCE

The body is of a Caucasian male who measures 73 inches, weighing 260 pounds, appearing older than stated age. Postmortem rigidity has passed at time of autopsy. Postmortem lividity is fixed on posterior surface of torso and extremities.

The arm span is 73½ inches.

The general external appearance of the anterior and posterior thorax, abdomen, and flanks is normal. A tattoo in black ink of a Celtic cross is located on the left shoulder. Tattoo photograph attached.

Dried blood on right hand and surrounding the laceration on chest.

CLOTHING

I removed and labeled the following articles of clothing: a thick, black long-sleeved shirt, gray T-shirt, underwear, black socks, jeans, and black leather shoes.

The front of the long-sleeved shirt and T-shirt were soaked in damp and dried blood.

EXTERNAL INJURY

There is a triangular laceration measuring 3 mm at base, 1 mm at apex, and 1.75 cm in length located inferior to the left areola and in the mid-clavicular line in a parallel direction with apex superiorly located. The edges of the laceration are smooth with little or no fraying.

No other external injuries noted.

INTERNAL EXAMINATION

Chest: Left chest cavity contains approximately 3000 cc of clotted and non-clotted blood. Right chest cavity contains approximately 25 cc of straw-colored serous fluid.

Exhibit 28 (cont.)

AUTOPSY REPORT

INTERNAL INJURY

Tract of wound passes between the fourth and fifth ribs, transects the pectoralis major and minor muscles, the external intercostal membrane, through the middle lobe of the left lung, and transected the pericardium and entered the left ventricle. It passes through the myocardium on the posterior surface at its deepest point. Approximately 3000 cc of clotted and non-clotted blood is noted in the left chest cavity as described above. Trajectory of the tract enters the anterior chest wall 3 cm inferior and medial to the nipple line. The tract makes an angle approximately 20 degrees cephalad to the transverse plane.

TOXICOLOGY REPORT

1) Blood

a) Ethanol 0.16 gm%.

b) Drugs: cocaine present at less than 0.2 mg/ml quantity not sufficient for further study.

2) Urine

a) Positive for cocaine, cocaine metabolite (ecgonine methyl ester), and cocaethylene, with negative EMIT barbiturates screen.

3) Ocular Fluid

a) Ethanol 0.16 gm%.

Lee Taylor, MD
Deputy Coroner Nita City, Nita

March 26, YR-1

Exhibit 29

Photo of Cross Tattoo

Exhibit 30

Wound Diagram (Front/Back)

NITA CITY CORONER'S OFFICE

FRONT/BACK DIAGRAM

Deceased:	Patrick J. Connor
DOD:	March 10, YR-1
Examiner:	Lee Taylor, M.D., Deputy Coroner
Date Examined:	March 10, YR-1

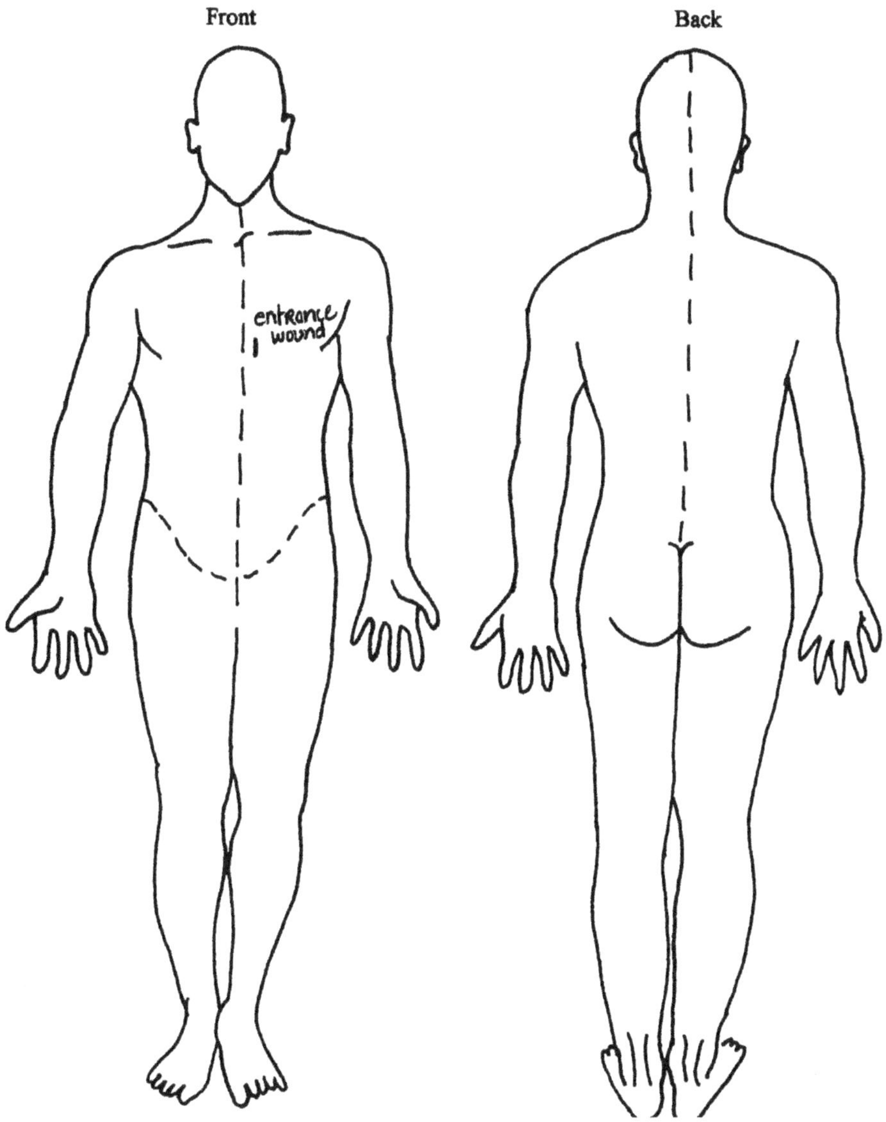

Exhibit 31

Wound Diagram (Lateral)

NITA CITY CORONER'S OFFICE

LATERAL DIAGRAM

Deceased:	Patrick J. Connor
DOD:	March 10, YR-1
Examiner:	Lee Taylor, M.D., Deputy Coroner
Date Examined:	March 10, YR-1

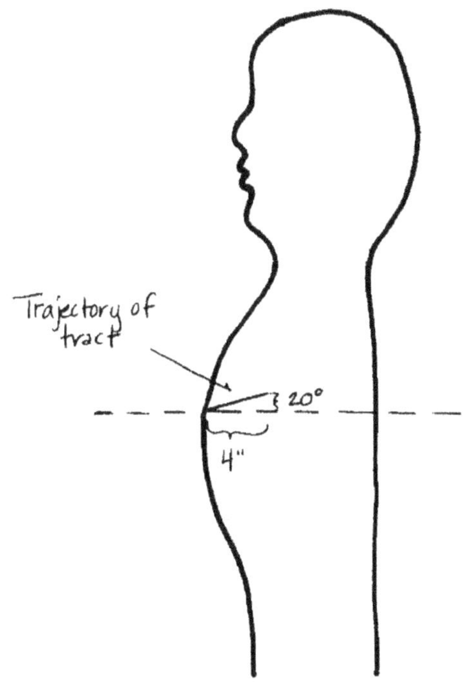

Exhibit 32

Coroner's Letter

NITA CITY CORONER'S OFFICE
245 Main Street
Nita City, Nita

March 27, YR-1

Detective Terry Hefler
Street Enforcement Unit
Nita City Police Department

Re: Deceased Patrick J. Connor, DOD: March 10, YR-1

Dear Detective Hefler:

I have enclosed a copy of the autopsy report for the deceased, Patrick J. Connor. The deceased suffered a single stab wound to the left ventricle of the heart. The path of the wound is at a slightly upward angle. I have enclosed diagrams reconstructing the entry of the blade. The diagrams are appended to the autopsy report.

I have determined to a high degree of certainty that the butterfly knife found at the scene was the weapon used to fatally stab Patrick Connor. I came to this conclusion because deceased's blood was found on the butterfly knife and the dimensions and blade edge characteristics of the butterfly knife are consistent with the fatal wound in deceased's chest.

At your request, I attempted to determine if the stab wound was likely caused by an offensive or defensive swing. I examined the knife, wound, deceased's physical characteristics, and information you provided me regarding Defendant Sanchez's physical characteristics. Unfortunately, the evidence is inconclusive on this issue. The generic and clean nature of the wound, without additional injuries, makes it impossible to characterize the wound as either offensive or defensive.

Please contact me if either your office or the prosecuting attorney needs additional information.

Sincerely,

L Taylor MD

Lee Taylor, MD
Deputy Coroner

Enclosures

Exhibit 33

Coroner's Résumé

LEE TAYLOR, MD
Deputy Coroner, Nita City, Nita

CURRICULUM VITAE

EDUCATION

YR-22–YR-20 **Residency: Boston Medical Examiner's Office**

- Specialization in Forensic Pathology
- Experience in over forty autopsies during residency

YR-26–YR-22 **Johns Hopkins School of Medicine**

- Specialization in Anatomic Pathology
- Graduated *cum laude*

YR-30–YR-26 **Boston College**

- BS Biology
- Graduated *magna cum laude*

PROFESSIONAL EXPERIENCE

YR-20–YR-15 **Assistant Pathologist: Maryland State Medical Examiner's Office**

- Performed over 100 autopsies
- Testified in sixteen cases, including ten murders

YR-15–Present **Deputy Coroner: Nita City Coroner's Office**

- Performed over 300 autopsies
- Testified in over thirty cases, including twenty murders
- Established residency rotation with Nita City Hospital

YR-5–Present **Adjunct Professor: Nita University**

- Courses include Introductory Pathology, Forensic Pathology, Microbiology

PROFESSIONAL ORGANIZATIONS

American Society for Clinical Pathology, American Society for Investigative Pathology, State Association of Medical Examiners, Forensic Science Society

PUBLICATIONS

"Choosing the Ideal Material for Tool Mark Test Impressions in Bone," *Journal of Forensic Sciences*, September YR-8.

"Determine the Instrument in Blunt Force Traumas," *Forensic Science Review,* June YR-4.

"What Is the Role of the Intern in the Modern Coroner's Office?" *Journal of Vocational Behavior,* May 25, YR-2.

Exhibit 34

Police Report, 4-12-YR-1, Immunity Deal

State of Nita **Narrative Report** NPR 5490 (Rev. 07-YR-10) OPI D87				Page 1 of 1
Date of Incident/Occurrence 03-10-YR-1	Time 3:00 PM	NCIC Number 68474	Officer I.D. Number 2653	Number 000YR-1-056
"X" One ☐ Narrative ☒ Supplemental	"X" One ☒ Criminal report ☐ Other	Type Supplemental ("X" Applicable) ☐ Collision Update ☒ Fatal ☐ Hit and Run Update ☐ Hazardous materials ☐ School bus ☐ Other ________		
City/County/Judicial District Nita City/Darrow/First			Reporting District/Beat Putnam Park	Citation Number N/A
Location/Subject Fisher's Convenience Store, 679 Old State Pike			State Highway Related ☐ Yes ☒ No	

NARRATIVE:

On April 12, YR-1, I met with Assistant United States Attorney Elizabeth McGraw, Assistant State's Attorney Erik Sullivan, Victor Buentello's attorney, and Victor Buentello at Ms. McGraw's office in Nita City. At this meeting we discussed the possibility of Buentello testifying against two defendants (Benjamin Carroll and Lester Moore) in case number A:YR-2cr00284, a federal prosecution for murder, arson, and racketeering charges. Buentello was one of two witnesses to the murder and has valuable information regarding the arson and racketeering charges. The federal case has nothing to do with the Las Calaveras gang or any other gang. Buentello is not a suspect in these federal crimes.

In exchange for his complete cooperation in the prosecution of Carroll and Moore, Ms. McGraw, with Mr. Sullivan's consent, offered Buentello immunity to the state charges of first-degree murder and participation in a criminal street gang in the stabbing death of Patrick Connor. Complete cooperation includes assistance in the preparation of the cases for trial and his testimony implicating Carroll and Moore in the federal murder, arson, and racketeering activities at their future trial.

Buentello asked how this agreement might impact his testimony on behalf of Ernesto Sanchez for the murder of Patrick Connor. The prosecuting attorneys told Buentello that he was free to testify for either side in the Sanchez prosecution but that the prosecution could use this deal to avoid prosecution for murder to impeach his credibility. Buentello's attorney argued that if he testified for the defense, this "deal" would not be proper impeachment. The attorneys argued the point for a few minutes and agreed to leave that decision to the trial judge in the Sanchez case.

Buentello conferred with his counsel and agreed to the deal.

By this agreement the criminal case was closed on Buentello in the stabbing death of Patrick Connor.

Trial for Carroll and Moore TBA.

Preparer's Name, Rank, Division, and I.D. Number	Date
Hefler, Terry, Detective, Street Enforcement Unit, 2653	***04-12-YR-1***

YR-10 654613

PRELIMINARY HEARING TESTIMONY
MARY KELLY

Direct Examination by the State

Q: What is your name?

A: Mary Kelly.

Q: When were you born?

A: November 11, YR-30.

Q: What is your address?

A: I live in Washington, DC, and would rather not give my full address.

Q: Do you work?

A: Yes, I work at a private school in DC. I teach fifth grade.

Q: Have you always lived in DC?

A: No, I used to live at 680 Old State Pike in Nita City. I lived there for seven years with a coworker named Sarah Collins.

Q: Where did you work?

A: Putnam Park Elementary.

Q: Tell me what happened on March 10, YR-1.

A: Well, I heard people shouting outside Fisher's Convenience Store. I couldn't understand what they were saying, but they sounded angry. Sarah had gone to the convenience store a few minutes earlier, so when I heard the loud voices, I walked out the front door and across my front yard to see what was going on and to make sure Sarah was all right.

Q: What happened next?

A: I got about halfway across my front yard when I could see a gang fight across the street in the parking lot of the convenience store.

Q: How many people were involved in the fight?

A: There were about thirty to thirty-five people involved.

Q: What did you do next?

A: Well, people were gathering along the front part of my yard to watch the fight, but I stayed in the middle of my yard. I was worried that Sarah had gotten caught up in the fight, but I spotted her standing in the front door of the convenience store with a few other people. She seemed safe enough.

Q: What happened after that?

A: I continued to watch the fight from about twenty-five yards away. That is when I saw the murder.

Q: What did you see?

A: I saw the victim with a baseball bat. He was walking toward Ernesto Sanchez. I've seen Sanchez around the neighborhood with the Las Calaveras bunch several times, and he must have tripped or something because he was on the ground.

Q: How did Mr. Sanchez get on the ground?

A: I didn't see how he got that way, but there wasn't anyone close enough to push him down.

Q: What happened next?

A: When the victim was about three feet from Sanchez, Victor Buentello jumped him from behind. Buentello grabbed the victim's arms and yanked them back over the guy's head. He pulled the victim off balance and caused him to drop the bat.

Q: And what happened next?

A: Buentello got the victim under control as Sanchez got up from the ground. They were sort of on the fringe of the fight, so I thought that Buentello might push the guy to the ground and walk away, but instead he held the guy while Sanchez stabbed him in the chest. The victim was defenseless.

Q: What did Sanchez use to stab the victim?

A: Sanchez used a small knife. He drove it straight into the victim's heart. The victim went down quickly.

Q: What happened after that?

A: Sanchez and Buentello ran. I got a good look at Sanchez's face because he cut through the corner of my yard.

Q: Did you see anything after that?

A: Yes, I saw this small, maybe five-foot tall, Las Calaveras guy standing a few feet away and watching the stabbing. He yelled, "SC down. Las Calaveras rules."

Q: What happened next?

A: The police arrived about two minutes later. Detective Hefler interviewed me at the scene.

Q: Was that the only time you spoke with Detective Hefler?

A: No, Detective Hefler came to my house a few days after the stabbing and showed me a bunch of photographs. Detective Hefler just asked me to look through the photographs and tell him if the guy involved in the stabbing was in the bunch.

Q: Did you recognize anyone in the photographs?

A: Yes, I easily picked out Sanchez because he's one of the ones who cut through my yard.

Q: Do you see the individual that stabbed Mr. Connor on March 10, YR-1?

A: Yes. He is at the defense table wearing a black suit.

Q: Please let the record reflect that Ms. Kelly has identified Ernesto Sanchez as the individual that stabbed Mr. Connor on March 10, YR-1.

COURT: It is so noted.

Cross-Examination by the Defense

Q: About five years ago, a lot of Latinos moved into your neighborhood?

A: Yes.

Q: And you thought these Latinos disrespected you, is that right?

A: Yes, especially the ones who belonged to Las Calaveras, the Latino gang that ran the neighborhood.

Q: And you thought they were rough and crude, right?

A: Yes.

Q: And these Latinos would harass you, correct?

A: Yes.

Q: And isn't it true that they would cut through your yard to get to Fisher's Convenience Store?

A: Yes, they would.

Q: And you thought that every Latino who wore red and white in your old neighborhood was bad news, right?

A: Yes, because they were all members of Las Calaveras.

Q: And Ms. Kelly, tell me how far away you were from the fight?

A: About twenty-five yards away.

Q: You did not see how Ernesto Sanchez fell to the ground?

A: No.

Q: Did you pay for airfare and lodging to testify here today?

A: No. The State paid for my airfare and hotel.

I certify that the foregoing document is a true and accurate transcription of Mary Kelly's preliminary hearing testimony, which was given under oath, administered by me, on July 29, YR-1, in *State v. Sanchez* in the District Court, Nita City, Nita.

Certified by:

Anna Doreen Dillon

Court Reporter

July 30, YR-1

Commission number: 2345

My commission expires: December 30, YR+2

State Expert's Case Analysis

Nita City Police Department

Nita City, Nita

"To Serve, Honor and Protect"

September 24, YR-1

Assistant State's Attorney
Office of the District Attorney for Nita City
Nita City, Nita

Re: Gang Murder Case—Patrick J. Connor, Deceased

Dear Assistant State's Attorney:

I am a lieutenant in the Nita City Street Enforcement Unit (NCSEU), Nita City Police Department. I am writing in response to your inquiry to the NCSEU for assistance in the prosecution of Ernesto Sanchez, and possibly Victor Buentello, for the murder of Patrick J. Connor.

For fifteen of my twenty-one years in the Nita City Police Department, I served in the NCSEU, a six-officer group that works to stop gang activities in Nita City. I helped found the NCSEU in response to the growing street crime problem in our community. I noticed that many young adults were forming or joining gangs and inflicting terror upon Nita City's store owners and citizens. I observed gang activities becoming increasingly violent and formed the NCSEU in response. The unit's goals are dual pronged. First, we aggressively pursue criminal prosecutions of gang members. Second, we help promote alternatives to gang membership through school information sessions, after-school programs, and job training.

To further these goals, I began the gang member database (GMD), the most comprehensive compilation of gang data in Nita. Based on our observations over the past fifteen years, NCSEU has compiled data on over 20 gangs and 700 gang members. Our database is not exhaustive but includes information on many of Nita City's most notorious and dangerous gangs, with specific information on individual gang colors, signs, and activities.

Before I joined the police force, I received an associate's degree in criminal justice from Nita Community College. During my fifteen years in the NCSEU, I received extensive formal training. I have attended numerous conferences and seminars on identifying and stopping gang activity. Just recently, I completed a three-month intensive anti-gang activity course sponsored by the FBI. I have also worked with undercover officers infiltrating a local gang named the 28th Street Disciples. I have testified twice as an expert in gang activities and membership. Both times I testified as an expert, I testified on behalf of the State. Those two prosecutions were of multiple 28th Street Disciples members. My assistance with the undercover operations and in-court testimony resulted in the successful prosecution of nineteen gang members, five of whom received life sentences. While working with the undercover officers in this case, I observed firsthand through around-the-clock surveillance the inner workings of an active gang. I learned about the code of silence, a fundamental characteristic of most gangs. I also observed two instances of gangs violently retaliating against gang members who broke the code of silence and "ratted out" gang members to police officers. Through my undercover experience I additionally learned that gangs have meetups that occur on a specific day of the week at different and distinct locations to avoid run-ins with law enforcement.

Based on the preliminary information I received about Ernesto Sanchez and Victor Buentello, I believe I can help you with a successful prosecution. Although I am not familiar with these two individuals personally and they do not appear in the GMD, I know quite a bit about the gang with which they associate, Las Calaveras. Las Calaveras is one of the largest and most violent gangs in Nita City, with approximately eighty members. Las Calaveras members are all of Latino decent. The gang itself has unusual origins. The gang began twelve years ago, not as violent "gangbangers" but as a local soccer club. The soccer club played most of its games on the weekends, after which it would gather for a post-game meal and other social activities. Las Calaveras players wore red and white uniforms and proudly displayed their colors. Soon thereafter, a dispute arose between Las Calaveras and a rival soccer club, and the violence began. Membership increased from the initial sixteen players on the soccer club. The police have arrested, and your office has successfully prosecuted, Las Calaveras members on a variety of criminal charges, including assault, assault with a deadly weapon, drug offenses, and theft. Our database contains information on twenty-four Las Calaveras gang members and contains extensive information about the gang. The gang still wears red and white clothing, usually soccer jerseys and warm-up pants and jackets. Gang members often, but not always, have a skull tattoo. Las Calaveras gang members meet at specific locations on Fridays every week. There are a few distinct locations that our GMD has tracked throughout the years since the gang's formation. Known meet-up locations for Las Calaveras gang members include Stingeni's Autoshop (5550 Iris Street), Herrera's Latin Cuisine (3233 Mason Square), Pena's Sports Club (2000 Padron Court), Sam and Taylor's Bodega (616 Clark Street), and Grey's Bait and Tackle (1001 Donoghue Street). The Friday meeting time can vary but the meetings generally take place around midnight.

I do not have as much information about the Stone Cross gang. They originated in New York City, and members started appearing in Nita City two years ago. Members of the Stone Cross, or SC as they are known, tend to be of Irish descent, but not always. They wear black and often have Celtic cross tattoos. They threaten small business owners with arson or other forms of vandalism if the business owner does not pay them a portion of their profits. I have not had any personal dealings with SC, and we only have nine members in the GMD. The deceased, Patrick J. Connor, was not listed in the GMD.

After reviewing the police and medical examiner's reports in this case, it is my opinion that Ernesto Sanchez and Victor Buentello are members of Las Calaveras. I reach this conclusion based on the following factors: 1) they live in the neighborhood predominantly associated with Las Calaveras; 2) they were involved in a group altercation with other established Las Calaveras members (including the leader of Las Calaveras, Jimmy "Papa Ru" Rueda); 3) they were wearing Las Calaveras colors at the time of the altercation; 4) they are Latino; 5) Sanchez was armed; 6) Buentello has a criminal record (including crimes associated with gang activity such as assault and vandalism); 7) a witness

(Martin Salas) identified Sanchez as a known Las Calaveras gang member; 8) Sanchez has frequently been seen around town with other gang members; 9) Detective Hefler found skull sketches, which are associated with the Las Calaveras gang, in Sanchez's bedroom; 10) they are known by gang monikers (Neto and B); and 11) I reviewed screenshots of Heart 24/7 app tracking data of Sanchez's phone.

Heart 24/7 is an app that tracks an individual's phone location as it travels from destination to destination and the length of time the phone was in that location. Federal courts across the country have found this tracking data to be sufficient and reliable when it comes to determining the exact location of the individual's phone. Heart 24/7 keeps records of the individual's trips from the previous two months and is mainly used by parents to track their children's locations. Screenshots from Sanchez's Heart 24/7 account locates his phone at several of the meet up locations on days that Las Calaveras members would have their meetups. The Heart 24/7 screenshots helped inform my opinion on Sanchez's Las Calaveras gang member status.

You can expect Sanchez and Buentello, as members of the same gang, to support each other's stories as to what happened in the fight. They most likely rehearsed their stories as soon as the murder occurred.

I hope this information helps in your prosecution of the two defendants. If I can lend further assistance, please do not hesitate to contact me.

Sincerely,

Jamie Delgado

Jamie Delgado

Defense Expert's Case Analysis

Date: October 5, YR-1

To: Counsel for Ernesto Sanchez

From: Pat Donahue,
Director, Nita City Anti-Gang Community Center

Subject: Sanchez and Buentello
Fisher's stabbing on March 10, YR-1

My name is Pat Donahue. I am a former gang member. Approximately twenty-four years ago, I started a gang called the Edmond Hill Posse in Nita City, Nita. As the leader, I stole, pushed drugs, vandalized property, and was an accessory to murder. For my crimes, I spent ten years in jail, and I deserved every second of it.

But jail changed me. I renounced my gang membership and was instrumental in disbanding the Edmond Hill Posse. During my time in jail, I began writing books for teenagers aimed at steering youth away from gangs and into more productive activities. I wrote and published six books and was nominated for a local peace prize for my literary efforts. Also, while I was in jail, I assisted the police in three gang investigations that led to the arrest and successful prosecution of eight gang members.

When I was released from jail in December YR-11, I decided that something needed to be done about gangs in our city. I noticed that children were joining gangs at an alarming rate, and many were headed down the same path that I once took. I began the Nita City Anti-Gang Community Center. The center allows me to continue what I started in jail. I have a staff of six counselors, all of whom are Nita-licensed social workers or youth counselors. Some of my staff members are also former gang members. We offer alternatives to gang activities, such as sports, music lessons, and academic tutoring. We also meet with and encourage active gang members to renounce their membership. So far, we have placed fourteen former gang members in legitimate jobs.

In conjunction with my work at the center, I earned my bachelor's degree in behavioral psychology with a minor in social work from Nita University. Following graduation, I enrolled in a master's degree program and now have an advanced degree, also from Nita University, in youth counseling. In addition to my work at the center, I counsel students at Nita City high schools. I have written numerous articles on gang activities, which have been published in *The New York Times* and *The Washington Post*. My book, *Gang Pressure*, was published in December YR-2 and is selling very well as a supplemental textbook in college courses on gang behavior. I have provided analysis and comments on approximately fifteen gang-related cases. Sometimes my analysis has been favorable to the prosecution's case, and sometimes it is more favorable to the defense—as it is in this case. I have never been paid for my case analysis services. I do it as a community service. I have never been called to testify on my conclusions; however, I have been asked to speak at numerous law enforcement seminars and conferences on my knowledge of gang membership and behavior.

Although I don't know Ernesto Sanchez and Victor Buentello personally, I am familiar with Las Calaveras. One former member of Las Calaveras completed the program at the center and renounced his gang membership. I remember his first name was Carlos, but I don't know where he lives now. I helped him remove his gang tattoo and subsequently found a job for him in Nita City. Las Calaveras is an active gang in Nita City with an estimated forty members. Las Calaveras members usually wear red and white warm-up jackets and pants. They also are branded with a simple skull tattoo. These skull tattoos are often homemade and crude. I have attached an example of a Las Calaveras skull tattoo.

Based on my extensive experience with Nita City gangs, I do not believe that Ernesto Sanchez and Victor Buentello belong to Las Calaveras. First, they do not have skull tattoos. This marker, I believe, is the most reliable indication of membership in Las Calaveras. Although Detective Hefler found skull sketches in Sanchez's bedroom, drawing skulls is not a known indicator for Las Calaveras membership. In fact, the drawings that were found in his bedroom are skull sketches related to the Mexican holiday, the Day of the Dead. Second, they were not wearing the typical red and white warm-up suits or soccer jerseys. Although they were both wearing red shirts, tell-tale indication of membership in Las Calaveras is red and white warm-up suits or soccer jerseys, not just red shirts. Third, neither Sanchez nor Buentello live in the Putnam Park Apartments. Putnam Park Apartments is the residence of nearly 75 percent of all Las Calaveras members. Fourth, the addresses that Sanchez's Heart 24/7 account pings him at on the Fridays in February and March are not all of the exact addresses where Las Calaveras members have their meetups. The screenshot locations of Sanchez's phone do not place him directly at the addresses of the different meetup locations. Additionally, it is impossible to determine an accurate time these gang meetups occur as they are quite random and there is no evidence that the gang met at these locations on those particular dates. Finally, Sanchez has no criminal record and is enrolled at Nita Community College. This would be highly unlikely for a gang member.

In my expert opinion, because Sanchez and Buentello lack the requisite characteristics for membership in Las Calaveras, I don't believe they are members of the gang. I believe they were merely in the wrong place at the wrong time.

I have less familiarity with the second gang involved in the March 10 incident. The Stone Cross, or SC, is a gang with approximately thirty members locally. The members of SC are not centralized in one neighborhood. SC is a New York City gang that is relatively new to Nita City. Their presence in Nita City only goes back a year or two. The common bond between SC members is Irish heritage. They are a rough group known to threaten shop owners. I met with an SC member about two weeks ago. I don't know his name or where he is now. He only came in for one counseling session, and I have not seen him since.

Please let me know if I can be of any assistance to you. If you do decide to use my expertise, I will not charge you for my consulting services, but I will charge you $100 per hour for the time I spend away from the center to testify in court. I will donate the fee to the center.

Exhibit 35

Photo of Skull Tattoo

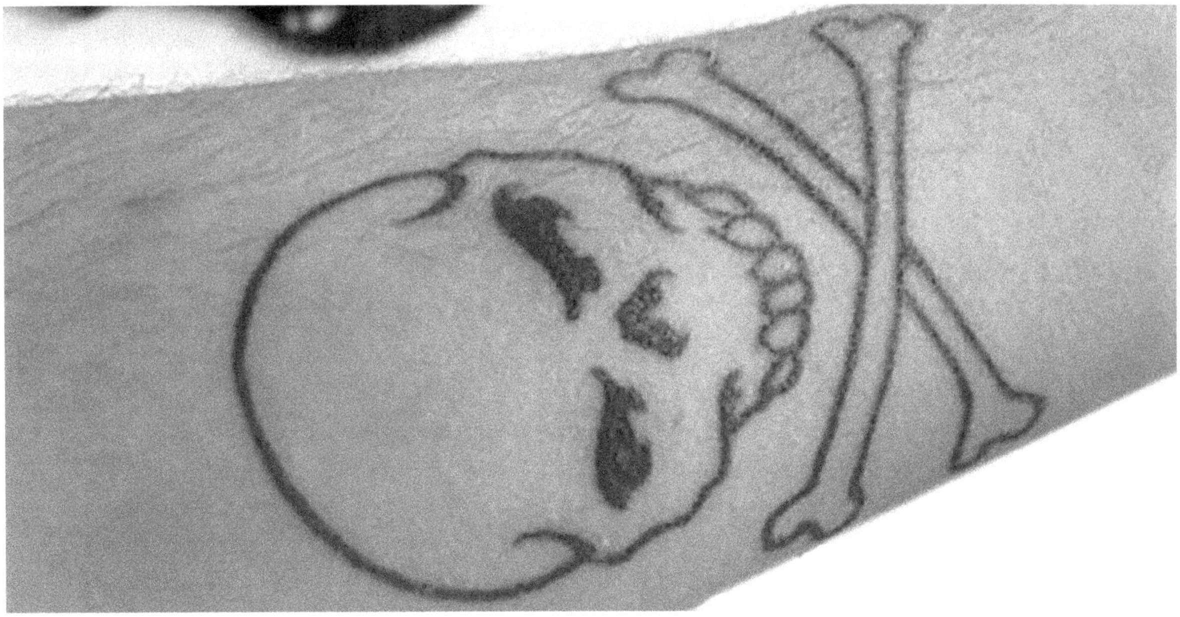

Exhibit 36

Screenshot of Defense Expert's Website

www.SAY NO TO NITA GANGS.ORG

Follow us!

HOME ABOUT US WHAT IS A CRIMINAL STREET GANG INFORMATION ANONYMOUSLY REPORT TO CRIME STOPPERS GET INVOLVED

About Us

To Members of the Nita Community:

Many of you know who I am, but for those who do not, let me introduce myself. My name is Pat Donahue, and I am a former gang member in Nita City. Twenty-three years ago, I became a gang member and helped start the Edmond Hill Posse, one of the most notorious gangs in Nita City history. I deeply regret the harm that I caused and now work to stop gang violence and membership from spreading.

Currently, I am the director of the Nita City Anti-Gang Community Center. I offer Nita City's youth an alternative to gang activity. The Center has organized sports teams, music lessons, and academic tutoring. We encourage youth to refrain from gang membership and stay in school. We also counsel gang members and support them if they renounce their gang membership. We find jobs for former gang members and even assist them in relocating their residences. I have even paid to have gang tattoos removed from former gang members who could not afford the procedure.

The Center is a wonderful place, but the fight against gangs starts at home. Parents must be informed of the signs to look for in their children. Are your kids distracted? Are their grades dropping in school? Are they wearing the same color clothing as their friends. Do they carry a weapon. THEY DO NOT HAVE TO HAVE A TATTOO TO BE GANG MEMBERS! Don't wait until it is too late.

I encourage you to drop by the Center. See what we are all about. We can help.

Sincerely,

Pat Donahue

RESOURCES

- Gangs and the Internet
- Kids and Gangs
- Gang Prevention Events
- Choosing Gang Life Can Be Fatal
- Female Ex-Gang Members Say No to Gangs at National Aboriginal Gang Conference

Exhibit 37

Defense Expert's Criminal Record

UNITED STATES DEPARTMENT OF JUSTICE
WASHINGTON, DC

Federal Bureau of Investigation

CRIMINAL ACTIVITY RECORD 10/30/YR-1

The following FBI record, NUMBER 362-827-P1, is furnished for OFFICIAL USE ONLY. Information shown on this identification record represents data furnished to the FBI by fingerprint contributors.

Subject: Pat Donahue

Date of Birth: 10/26/YR-40

Id. No.: 8-1263-772

Contributor of Record Information	Name	Arrested or Received	Charge	Disposition
Nita City, Nita	Pat Donahue	3/16/YR-26	Felony Larceny	Found Guilty; Juvenile Ct 6/24/YR-26
Nita City, Nita	Pat Donahue	7/5/YR-26	Felony Larceny (Conviction 3/16/YR-26)	Sentenced, 18 mos. Juvenile Detention
Statesville, Nita	Pat Donahue	9/4/YR-24	Misdemeanor Vandalism	Fined $500
New Orleans, Louisiana	Pat Donahue	5/21/YR-23	Felony Burglary	Released; No charges
Nita City, Nita	Pat Donahue	8/19/YR-22	Felony Conspiracy to Murder	Found Guilty; Nita Trial Court 11/2/YR-22
Nita City, Nita	Pat Donahue	1/30/YR-21	Felony Conspiracy to Murder (Conviction 8/19/YR-21)	Sentenced, 10–15 yrs. Nita State Prison

Exhibit 38

Defense Expert's Memorandum to File

MEMO TO THE SANCHEZ AND BUENTELLO FILE

Ernesto Sanchez's attorney mentioned to me that Lieutenant Jamie Delgado was working with the State as an expert in gang activities and membership. I called Lieutenant Delgado on October 3, YR-1, to discuss his analysis and conclusions regarding the gang membership of Sanchez and Buentello. Lieutenant Delgado refused to discuss the case with me. He refused to provide me with any documentation of his analysis of this case. Lieutenant Delgado stated I should obtain his analysis through defense counsel.

He went a step further and stated that he was aware of my criminal record. He specifically stated that he knew I was convicted of conspiracy to commit murder for giving the name, contact information, and work schedule of the victim to the gang member who took the victim's life. I did not argue with his recollection of the crime because it was true, but I reminded him that the crime occurred more than twenty years ago. I informed him of my education and hard work on anti-gang efforts. I asked him if he had taken the time to visit the Nita City Anti-Gang Community Center. He said he had no interest in my center and that I would always be a criminal to him.

I informed him that I had reviewed the Sanchez and Buentello case thoroughly and did not believe that they were gang members. I assured him that no amount of personal attacks from him against me would change my conclusions.

Pat Donahue, 10-3-YR-1

Exhibit 39

Butterfly Knife Operations

Nita City Police Department

Nita City, Nita

"To Serve, Honor and Protect"

To: **Assistant State's Attorney**

From: **Detective Terry Hefler, Nita City Police Department**

Re: **Butterfly Knife Operating Procedures**

The butterfly knife, also known as the balisong knife, is a folding pocketknife with two handles. To open the knife, one must unlock the latch and counter-rotate the handles around the blade. When the knife is closed, the handles hide the blade. This makes the knife safe to carry in a pocket.

To an inexperienced user, opening and operating the butterfly knife can be slow and cumbersome. On the other hand, trained users can quickly bring forth the blade with one hand in a quick, fluid motion. An experienced user could produce the blade from a closed and locked position in less than three seconds.

Attached is a photograph composite of the opening operations of a butterfly knife. I used a butterfly knife of the same size and construction as the butterfly knife used in the Connor murder.

Exhibit 40

Composite Photo of Butterfly Knife Operations

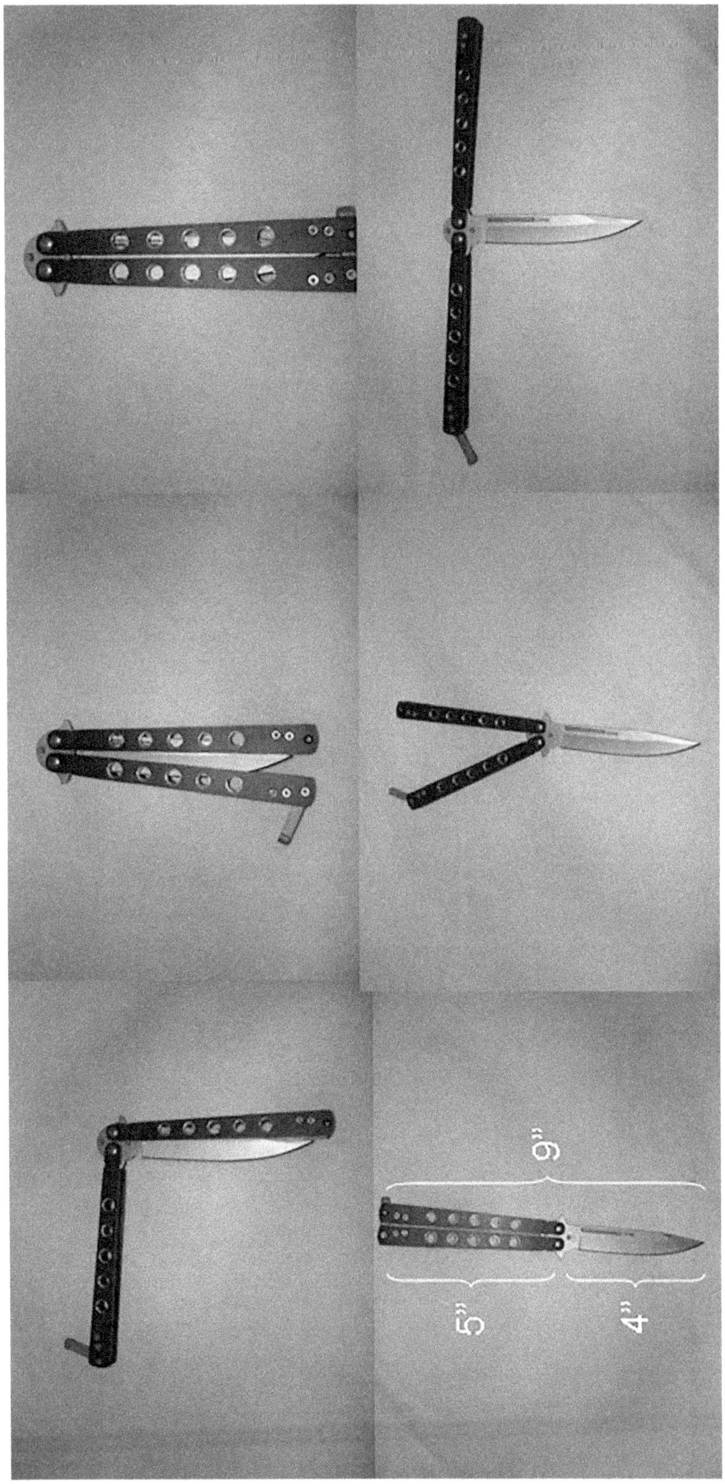

Exhibit 41

Information about Day of the Dead

Related Material

(THIS IS NOT EVIDENCE)

INFORMATION ON SKULL SKETCHES

Cultural Importance of Skulls

Skulls have great significance in Mexican culture. A skull is a powerful symbol that represents both death and rebirth. Skulls, or *calaveras*, are a staple of one of the most widely recognized Mexican holidays—Dia de los Muertos, the Day of the Dead.

Dia de los Muertos

Dia de los Muertos is a four-day holiday celebrated each year in Mexican culture to honor the deceased relatives and the afterlife. All over Mexico, individuals paint their faces and decorate skulls with intricate and colorful detail in celebration of their ancestors. These decorated skulls are often reflected as a gift or offering the spirit of the deceased and placed on altars in remembrance of lost loved ones.

Poems, also called "calaveras," relate to the Day of the Dead. For more information, visit https://en.wikipedia.org/wiki/Literary_Calavera.

Exhibit 42

Heart 24/7 Screenshots

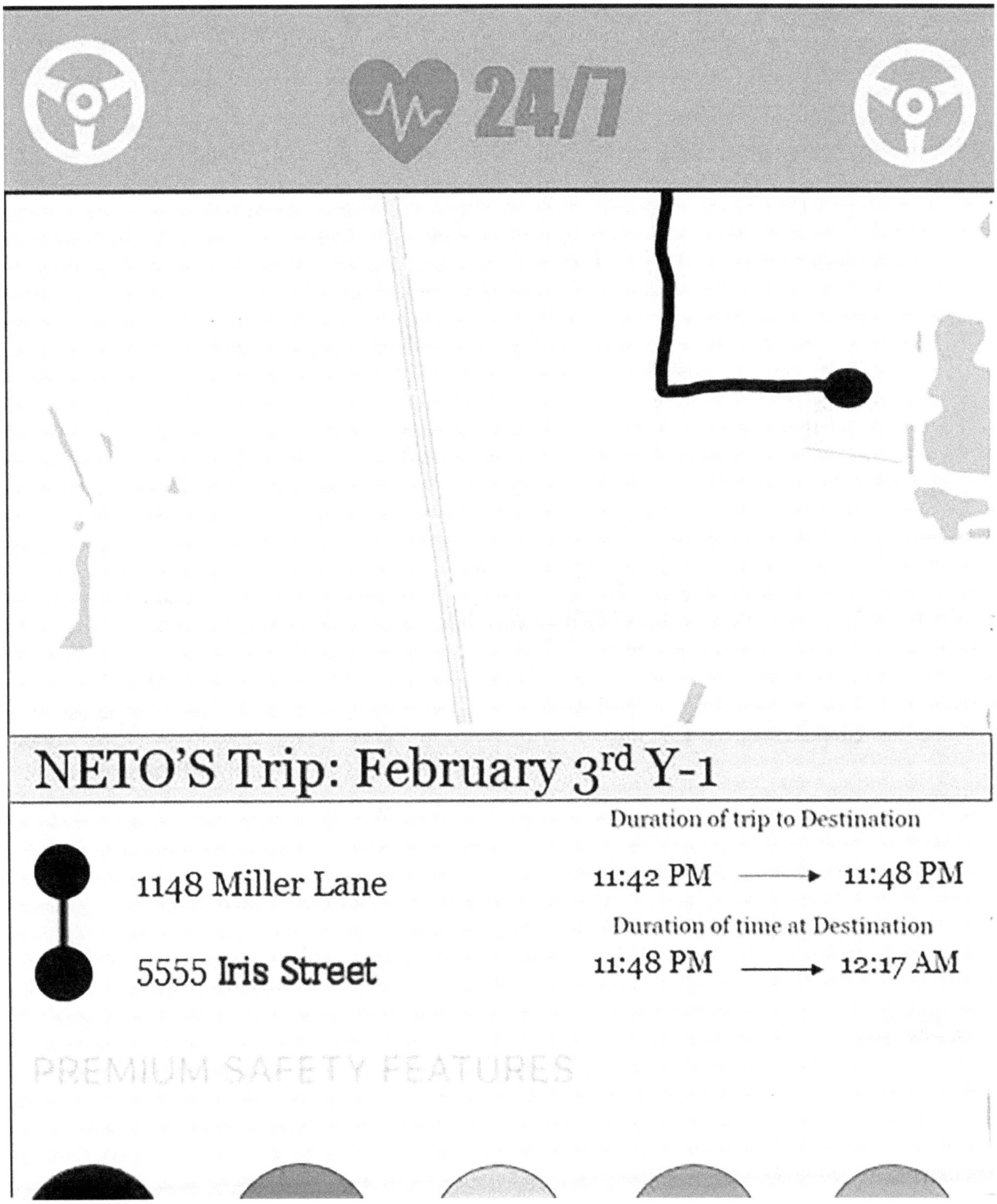

NETO'S Trip: February 10th Y-1

	Duration of trip to Destination
1148 Miller Lane	2:00 PM ⟶ 2:11 PM
	Duration of time at Destination
3233 **Mason Square**	2:11 PM ⟶ 2:58 PM

PREMIUM SAFETY FEATURES

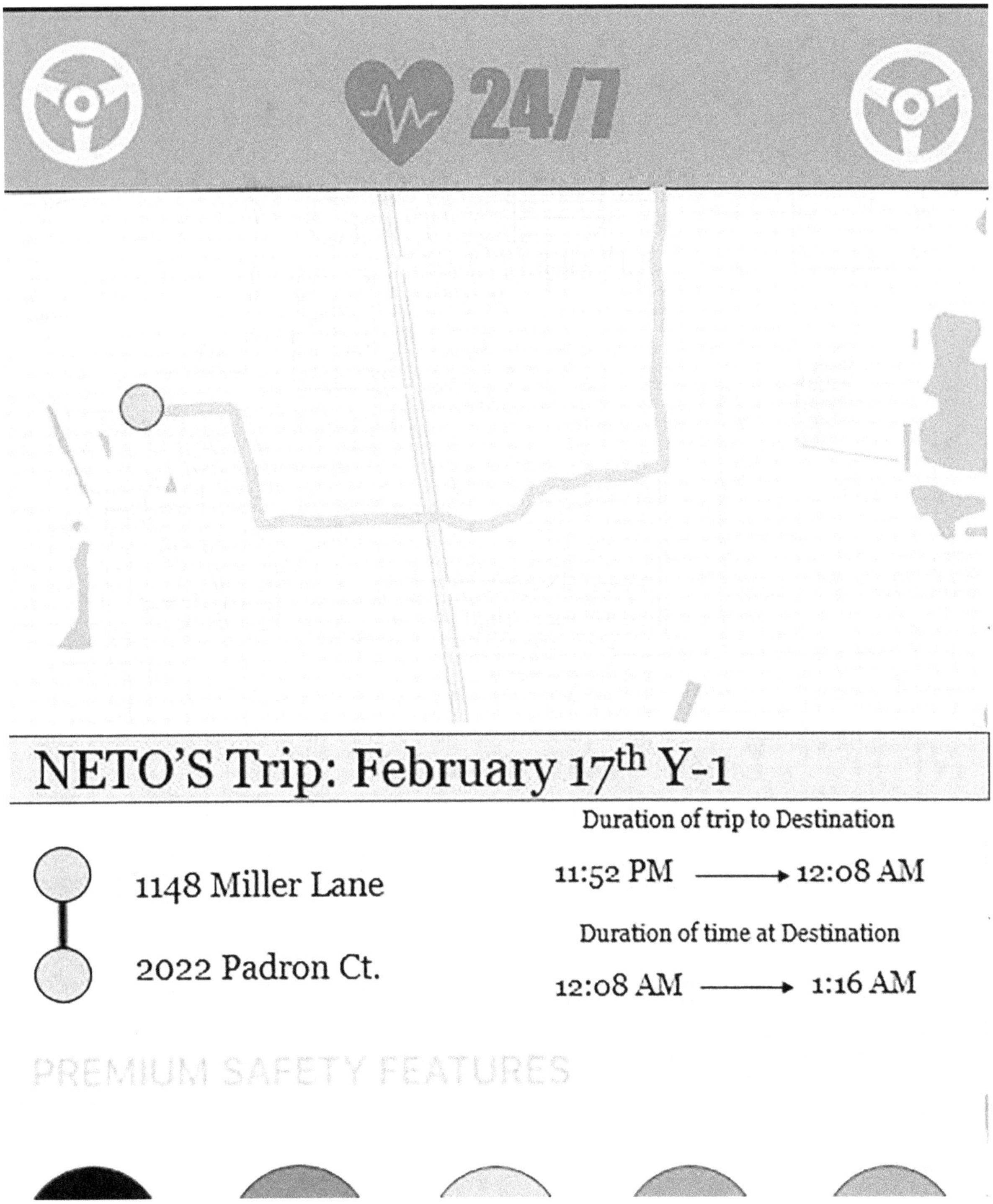
24/7
NETO'S Trip: February 17th Y-1
Duration of trip to Destination
1148 Miller Lane
11:52 PM → 12:08 AM
Duration of time at Destination
2022 Padron Ct.
12:08 AM → 1:16 AM
PREMIUM SAFETY FEATURES

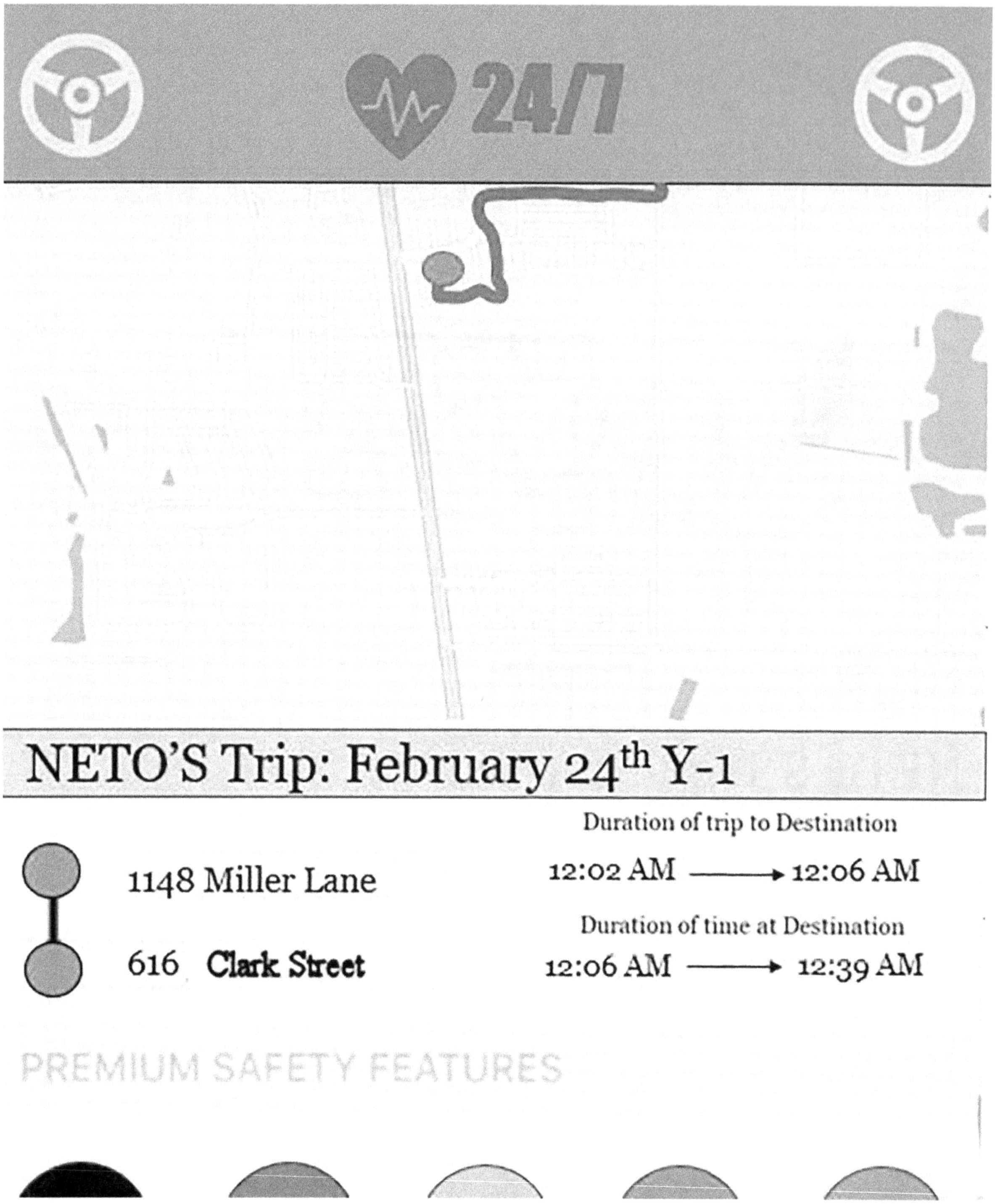
24/7
NETO'S Trip: February 24th Y-1
Duration of trip to Destination
1148 Miller Lane
12:02 AM → 12:06 AM
Duration of time at Destination
616 Clark Street
12:06 AM → 12:39 AM
PREMIUM SAFETY FEATURES

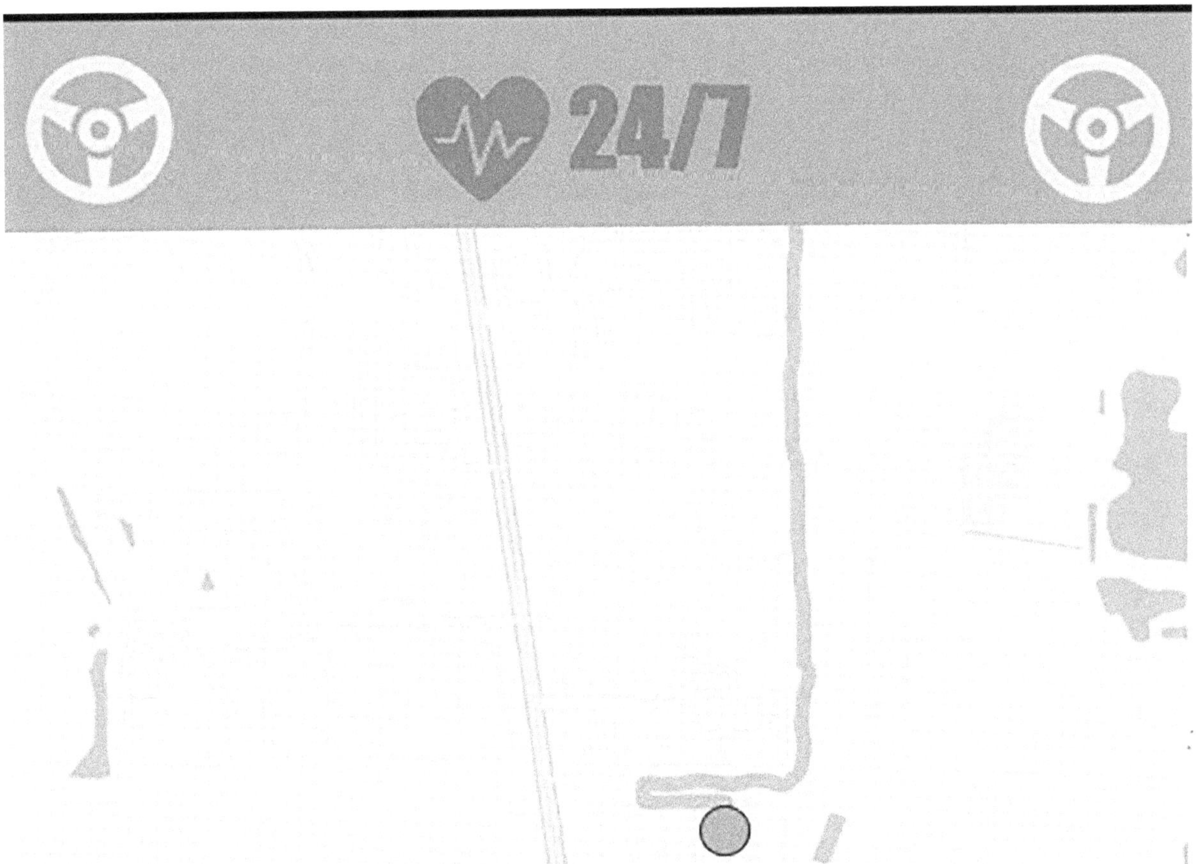

NETO'S Trip: March 8th Y-1

	Duration of trip to Destination
1148 Miller Lane	10:57 PM ⟶ 11:11 PM
	Duration of time at Destination
2022 Sargent Lane	11:11 PM ⟶ 12:43 AM

PREMIUM SAFETY FEATURES

Case Law and Jury Instructions

Nita Case Law

Affirmative Defenses: Self-Defense. Nita Supreme Court.

State v. Zimmerman, 11 Nita 90 (YR-15). The criminal case law in Nita is well settled: for affirmative defenses such as self-defense, the burden of proof is on the State. The defendant has the burden of raising the defense and presenting some evidence to support the defense, but once that is done, the burden shifts to the State to prove each element of the crime charged, including that the defendant did not act in self-defense.

Affirmative Defenses: Imperfect Self-Defense. Nita Supreme Court.

State v. King, 10 Nita 645 (YR-17). The criminal case law in Nita does not recognize the formal theory of imperfect self-defense as a viable affirmative defense. In *King*, the defendant killed an individual while holding an actual, but unreasonable, belief that the individual posed an imminent threat. The court determined that the defendant actually believed the individual intended deadly harm, but the individual in fact intended non-deadly harm. Because the defendant held an unreasonable belief, the defense of self-defense was not available to the defendant. As an alternative to complete self-defense, the defendant asserted imperfect self-defense. The court held that Nita does not recognize imperfect self-defense as an affirmative defense.

Unlawful Carrying of a Concealed Weapon. Nita Supreme Court.

State v. McMurray, 7 Nita 2d 5 (YR-6). Under Nita Criminal Code Section 2-43-201, a defendant who knowingly carries about his person a knife that is four inches long, not in an open manner fully exposed to view, is not guilty of the crime of unlawful carrying of a concealed weapon. The plain language of the statute suggests that the legislature did not intend for "a knife that is four inches long" to be regulated under the statute.

Proposed Jury Instructions

These instructions are taken from the Nita Model Jury Instructions and reflect the current law of Nita.

1) Members of the jury: You have been selected and sworn in as jurors. You must arrive at your verdict by unanimous vote. You must base your verdict on the facts and the law. First, you must determine the facts from the evidence presented in the trial and not from any other source. Second, you must accept and follow the law as I state it to you, regardless of whether you agree with it.

2) The State of Nita has charged the defendant with the crimes of first-degree murder and participation in a criminal gang. The defendant has pleaded not guilty.

3) Under the criminal code of the State of Nita, a person commits the crime of first-degree murder if they commit a willful, deliberate, and premeditated killing.

   "Willful" means the defendant actually intended to kill the victim.

   "Deliberate" means formed or arrived at as a result of thought and weighing of considerations for and against the proposed course of action.

   "Premeditated" means killing after consciously deciding to do so. The law does not fix the exact period of time that must pass between the formation of the premeditated intent to kill and the killing. The period of time must be long enough to allow reflection by the defendant. The premeditated intent to kill must be formed before the killing.

4) To prove the crime of first-degree murder, the state must prove the following propositions:

   a) That the victim, Patrick Connor, is dead;

   b) That the conduct of the defendant caused the death of Patrick Connor; and

   c) That the killing of Patrick Connor was willful, deliberate, and premeditated.

   If you find from your consideration of all the evidence that each of these propositions has been proved beyond a reasonable doubt, then you should find the defendant guilty of first-degree murder.

   If, on the other hand, you find from your consideration of all the evidence that any of these propositions has not been proven beyond a reasonable doubt, then you should find the defendant not guilty of first-degree murder.

5) Under the criminal code of the State of Nita, a person commits the crime of participation in a criminal street gang if he actively participates in a criminal street gang with knowledge

that the members are engaged in, or have engaged in, a pattern of criminal gang activity, and who willfully promotes, furthers, or assists in any felonious criminal conduct by members of that gang.

"Criminal street gang" means any organization of three or more persons, with the following two characteristics:

a) having as one of its activities the commission of one or more of the following criminal acts:

   i) Unlawful homicide or manslaughter;

   ii) Robbery;

   iii) Assault with a deadly weapon;

   iv) Rape;

   v) The sale or possession for sale of controlled substances; and

b) having a common name or common identifying sign or symbol.

"Pattern of criminal gang activity" means the commission of or attempted commission of two or more of the following crimes:

   i) Unlawful homicide or manslaughter;

   ii) Robbery;

   iii) Assault with a deadly weapon;

   iv) Rape;

   v) The sale or possession for sale of controlled substances

"Active participation" means that the person must have a relationship with the criminal street gang that is more than passive or inactive.

6) To prove the crime of participation in a criminal street gang, the state must prove the following propositions:

   a) That the defendant actively participated in a criminal street gang;

   b) That members of the criminal street gang engaged in or have engaged in a pattern of criminal gang activity;

c) That the defendant knew that the gang members engaged in or have engaged in a pattern of criminal gang activity; and

d) That the defendant directly committed or aided and abetted another member of that gang in committing the crime of murder.

If you find from your consideration of all the evidence that each of these propositions has been proven beyond a reasonable doubt, then you should find the defendant guilty of participation in a criminal street gang.

If, on the other hand, you find from your consideration of all the evidence that any of these propositions has not been proved beyond a reasonable doubt, then you should find the defendant not guilty of participation in a criminal street gang.

7) Self-defense is a complete defense. You are required to find the defendant not guilty if all of the following four factors are present:

a) The defendant was not the aggressor;

b) The defendant believed that he was in immediate and imminent danger of death or serious bodily harm;

c) The defendant's belief was reasonable; and

d) The defendant used no more force than was necessary to defend himself in light of the threatened or actual force.

The defendant has introduced evidence that he killed Patrick Connor in self-defense. To convict the defendant of murder, the State must prove that the defendant did not act in self-defense. If the defendant did act in self-defense, then the verdict for murder in the first or second degree must be not guilty.

To convict the defendant of voluntary manslaughter, the state must prove that the killing of Patrick Connor was unlawful. If the defendant's conduct was justifiable or excusable, the killing was lawful. If the defendant did act in self-defense, then the killing of Patrick Connor was lawful and the verdict for voluntary manslaughter must be not guilty.

8) *Expert Testimony.* You heard testimony in this case from witnesses with special knowledge, skill, experience, training, or education in a particular subject. These types of witnesses are referred to as expert witnesses. In determining what weight to give to the testimony of the expert witnesses, you should consider the qualifications and believability of the witness, the facts upon which each opinion is based, and the reasons for each opinion. You are not bound by the opinion of any expert witness. Give each opinion the weight you find it deserves. You may disregard any opinion if you find it to be unreasonable.

9) *Direct and Circumstantial Evidence.* The law recognizes two kinds of evidence—direct and circumstantial. *Direct evidence* proves a fact directly without further need for other evidence. In other words, the evidence by itself, if true, establishes the fact. The testimony of an eyewitness is a common example of direct evidence.

   Circumstantial evidence is a fact or circumstance which, if proven, provides a basis for a reasonable inference of another fact or facts. Circumstantial evidence proves a fact indirectly in that it follows from other facts or circumstances according to common sense, experience, and observations in life. Human footprints are an example of circumstantial evidence that a person was present.

   The law makes no distinction between direct and circumstantial evidence as to the degree or amount of proof required, and each should be considered according to whatever weight or value it may have. All of the evidence, direct and circumstantial, should be considered and evaluated by you in arriving at your verdict.

Instructions on Lesser Included Offenses

Murder in the Second Degree

If you are not satisfied beyond a reasonable doubt that the defendant is guilty of the crime of which he is accused and you unanimously so find, you may convict him of any lesser crime, provided you are satisfied beyond a reasonable doubt that he is guilty of that crime.

The law requires that each and every element of the offense be proven beyond a reasonable doubt before you may return a verdict of guilty of second-degree murder. Under the State of Nita's Criminal Code, a person commits the crime of second-degree murder if:

1) They intentionally, but not after deliberation, cause the death of a person; or

2) They intend to do great bodily harm to another person and the death of that person or different person is the result; or

3) They act with the intent to create a very high risk of death or great bodily harm with knowledge that death or great bodily harm is the probable result, and a death of the person does result.

As long as each of you believes that the defendant acted with one of these states of mind at the time of the alleged killing and as long as each of the other elements are proven beyond a reasonable doubt, the prosecution has met its burden of proof in this case. It is not necessary that all of you agree unanimously on which of the three states of mind the defendant possessed so long as each of you agree that he possessed one of the three states of mind.

Voluntary Manslaughter

The law requires that each and every element of the offense be proved beyond a reasonable doubt before you may return a verdict of guilty of voluntary manslaughter.

Every person who unlawfully kills another human being without malice aforethought, but either with intent to kill or with conscious disregard for human life, is guilty of voluntary manslaughter. There is no malice aforethought if the killing occurred upon a sudden quarrel or heat of passion or in the actual but unreasonable belief in the necessity to defend oneself or another person against imminent peril to life or great bodily injury.

Under the Criminal Code of the State of Nita, a person commits the crime of voluntary manslaughter if:

1) A human being was killed;

2) The killing was unlawful;

3) The perpetrator of the killing either intended to kill the alleged victim, or acted in conscious disregard for human life; and

4) The perpetrator's conduct resulted in the unlawful killing. A killing is unlawful, if it was neither justifiable nor excusable.

To reduce a killing upon a sudden quarrel or heat of passion from murder to voluntary manslaughter, the killing must have occurred while the slayer was acting under the direct and immediate influence of the quarrel or heat of passion. Where the influence of the sudden quarrel or heat of passion has ceased to obscure the mind of the accused, and sufficient time has elapsed for angry passion to end and for reason to control his conduct, it will no longer excuse express or implied malice, and reduce the killing to voluntary manslaughter. The question, as to whether the cooling period has elapsed and reason has returned, is not measured by the standard of the accused, but the duration of the cooling period is the time it would take the average or ordinarily reasonable person to have cooled the passion, and for that person's reason to have returned.

If you find from your consideration of all the evidence that this proposition has been proven beyond a reasonable doubt, then you should find the defendant guilty of voluntary manslaughter.

IN THE DISTRICT COURT
FOR THE CITY OF NITA

THE PEOPLE OF THE STATE OF NITA	)	
	)	
v.	)	Case No. CR 3711
	)	
ERNESTO P. SANCHEZ,	)	VERDICT
	)	
Defendant.	)	

We, the jury, return the following verdict, and each of us concurs in this verdict:

[Choose the appropriate verdict]

I. NOT GUILTY

We, the jury, find the defendant, Ernesto P. Sanchez, NOT GUILTY of all charges.

____
Presiding Juror

II. GUILTY

We, the jury, find the defendant, Ernesto P. Sanchez, GUILTY of the crime of:

_______Participation in a Criminal Street Gang

III. GUILTY

We, the jury, find the defendant, Ernesto P. Sanchez, GUILTY of the crime of:

_______Murder in the First Degree

_______Murder in the Second Degree

_______Voluntary Manslaughter

____
Presiding Juror

www.ingramcontent.com/pod-product-compliance
Lightning Source LLC
LaVergne TN
LVHW082344200926
848481LV00012B/3442